DECISION POINT

THE FIRST BOOK YOU READ
IF YOU WANT TO SUCCEED

NATHAN JOHN

authorHOUSE®

AuthorHouse™ UK
1663 Liberty Drive
Bloomington, IN 47403 USA
www.authorhouse.co.uk
Phone: UK TFN: 0800 0148641 (Toll Free inside the UK)
        UK Local: 02036 956322 (+44 20 3695 6322 from outside the UK)

Published by AuthorHouse 12/08/2020

ISBN: 978-1-6655-8275-9 (sc)
ISBN: 978-1-6655-8276-6 (hc)
ISBN: 978-1-6655-8274-2 (e)

Print information available on the last page.

Decision Point
The First Book You Read If You Want to Succeed

To all who know or have spoken with me, I have likely learned something from you, but specifically to my wife Emma, for her support for over twenty years. Thank you.

CONTENTS

"Success is measured by your happiness"

INTRODUCTION

This book is strong medicine! "Obsessed is the word lazy people use to describe the dedicated." (I don't know who said it, but spare a thought for it.)

You've done it! You've finished the exam, closed that big deal, completed the marathon, been promoted, or dropped a dress size. This fantastic success was all a result of first reaching a decision point, a decision you first made weeks, months, or even years ago. It doesn't matter. You made a decision.

OK, so we are jumping the gun a little bit, but these achievements and outcomes are real and can be real for you. You have made the decision to read this book, which is a great start in getting things back on track. Don't feel bad. Life often gets in the way of us, and there is never a good time to start reaching for our goals. We all fall foul of forgetting how to make good decisions and then having the discipline to stick to them.

Do not worry. You have taken an important step. You have made an important decision not to buy this book. (I wouldn't be so presumptuous.) No, you made a decision before that. You understand on one level or another that you are not happy with the status quo, your life as it is right now isn't what you wanted it to be, and you want to improve something in yourself or your life for a better future.

This was the important decision you made. How does it feel? You are that bit closer on your individual journey of personal development, your mindset has changed, you are ready to commit, and you are ready to back yourself and put your improvement first for a change. It feels amazing doesn't it.

So what makes this book different? How is this book going to help you? What is this book for? *Decision Point* is a fitting addition to the already expansive body of work in the personal development genre, specifically focusing on motivation and discipline. It sits among timeless and legendary authors, including some of my favorites, Napoleon Hill and Jim Rohn, and more contemporary writers, including the great Tony Robbins and Les Brown. In truth, this book is a little bit more. It is part self-help tool and part memoir of my own experiences, and I hope to form the foundation that you will go on to build in support of your lifelong personal development.

Decision Point is a tool for you to open the aperture on the opportunities that present themselves to you every day, and for you to exploit the very skill sets that are already in you. We are all blessed with the same twenty-four hours in a day, and I know that as a reader of this book, you have the internal drive to want more from your twenty-four hours. So I promise that before you turn the last page, you will have learned something new and be stronger-willed and mentally agile, with a plan of not only what you want to do next but how you are going to do it. You will have developed enough to make a life-changing decision.

From my own research and experiences, all you need to succeed is already in you. Some sceptics will cite luck as being a factor. I say that is total BS and offers those who don't believe in themselves an easy way out, a cheap excuse. By the time you reach the end of chapter 2, you won't believe in luck either, and as you pass by each chapter, your self-belief will grow exponentially. I will show you the simple yet powerful tools that you need to shape your own future the way you want it.

Decision Point will guide you into identifying what success means to you and giving you a road map to achieving those very dreams you have cast adrift and goals you had never dared dream. *Decision Point* should be used to shine a light on your own experiences, to focus your mind and give you tangible and realistic goals that will enable you to present the best version of yourself to the world and to have a positive impact on those around you.

I have written this book over years, but not because I am lazy or a procrastinator (actually that's not strictly true, I do sometimes, but we're all human), but because as I learned new skills and information and had more life-enhancing experiences, I couldn't leave them out of this text. I would feel like I was robbing you of the full experience as well as concepts and systems that have helped me, and I believe they will propel you toward your goals quicker than ever before. Alas, I have had to draw the line somewhere, but I am already teeming with ideas that I will share with you.

At some point, we all suffer from an absence of motivation, and that's fine. It's one of the many parts that make up the human condition. But what is most important is for you to recognise it and to recognise that you're not presenting the best version of yourself to those around you. And as such, you do yourself a huge injustice. This lack of motivation pulls at your enthusiasm to be creative and pursue life goals, and I'm certain that this same inertia paralyses thousands of prospective entrepreneurs, writers, artists, authors, sportsmen, and women the world over. Identify this and fight it with everything you have. It is not easy, but it's a fight you must win.

While some of my inspiration has come from world leaders in leadership, motivation, and personal development, I have been influenced by many teachers both in my day-to-day life as well as being in the most unlikely of situations. Over the past fifteen years, I have been presented with countless opportunities but was simply not equipped to recognise them. Some of those lessons I will be alluding to later.

One old Chinese proverb, "When the student is ready, the teacher will appear," immediately springs to mind. I recall when this proverb revealed its meaning to me back in 2012. No doubt you have heard it several times, but if, like me, you paid it passing lip service as a throwaway quip, then, also like me, you simply were not ready.

"Not ready for what?" you may ask.

The answer to that is simple: your own development.

I have taken decisions and made mistakes, but after gradually nurturing and growing my motivation, by strengthening my discipline, opening my eyes to opportunity, and focusing my energy on specific targets, I found that success is a by-product of simple processes. This is the secret sauce in *Decision Point*, the key takeaway, and I will reveal how to strengthen your disciplines for your ultimate success because the contingent factor on whether or not you succeed is not out there in the big, wide world. It is to what extent you believe that you can succeed. Focus is a simple five-letter word but an ever-increasingly difficult thing to do in today's modern world, littered with distractions. Focus is critical to your success.

Prepare for our first allegory. Imagine washing your car with a water hose, with the nozzle twisted all the way to the right. The spray is wide, and a fine mist covers your car. What happens when you twist the nozzle on the hose all of way to the left? The water jet becomes tighter, more focused, and stronger and goes further. The fine mist does get the car wet but doesn't ever really get the dirt off the surface. The wind can blow and influence the mist, but the jet or your attention and attitude, in this case, can saturate wherever it is focused and will blast away the dirt, leaving you with a shiny, clean car. Just like you on your journey to success, you will go further with focus.

Did that work for you? OK, how about another way to think about focus? Imagine you are shipwrecked on a desert island with nothing but some simple supplies, including some fishing equipment. So motivated by the hunger pains and knowledge that you need to eat to keep your strength up, you set out to go fishing on some rocks overlooking the sea. A bumper catch of fish reward your efforts, and you walk back to your camp to tuck into your freshly caught fish that afternoon.

In your supply kit, you find a magnifying glass. You have a brainwave. You will be able to make a fire to cook your fish by burning a pile of leaves and kindling. So you sit there moving your magnifying glass across the leaves to try to encourage a flame. Nothing happens, and nothing ever will as long as you are moving the magnifying glass, and thus the sun's rays, across the leaves. But as soon as you keep the magnifying glass still and focus, you harness the sun's power and see a single leaf begin to smoulder. Before you know it, the whole pile bursts into flames. Voila! Barbequed fish!

This is the power of focus, and this is what this book will leave you with as you turn the final page. The more you focus, the more incredible your results will be.

I have written this book to help you pick a starting point. After all, you've made a decision. So now we need to think about where the best place to start is. I have designed *Decision Point* to help you find a clear path from your idea, through to what you have chosen as your final destination, your own metric for success.

Your journey through the pages will be stimulating and, I hope, a thought-provoking experience. Fill the margins with notes. Get out a highlighter and underline bits that resonate. Put sticky notes on pages you want to come back to. Take quotes and post them on your social media. Share them with family and friends. Let everybody know how focused you are. You might be surprised how motivating positive feedback and accountability can be. For my part of the bargain, I will be your guide on reaching, taking, and, most importantly, delivering on your decision point. Here is a brief snapshot of what's to come over the next eight chapters.

Your Author

From experience, the number-one factor determining if you will reach your goals is the extent that you will consistently maintain your disciplines. You can't decide to be disciplined on Tuesdays and Wednesdays or when your favourite TV show is over. That is the polar opposite of what we are trying to achieve.

Discipline is the mastery of your own being, which includes both your mind and your body. Only when the two are totally aligned and in sync can you fully achieve your preset goals. This book offers some insight and enlightenment as to what makes discipline so difficult and offers some practical steps on what you can do to make discipline more of a routine activity in your daily life.

As you journey through these pages, I hope to stretch and elevate your thinking, tuning you to recognise aimless opinions instead of offering advice that you can choose to accept or reject based on its credibility and merit. I have learned that, broadly speaking, those with surface-level opinions, sound bites who probably spend their leisure time on social media, are unqualified and can largely be ignored. This kind of opinionated person will say things like, "Why are you reading that book? Those motivational books are all the same. They never work. You're wasting your time." And worst of all, they're telling you why you should not pursue your goals!

Think about this:

- Would you trust your financial future by taking the advice of a poor person?

- Would you take relationship advice from a multiple divorcée?
- When you have a medical issue, would you take the opinion of your postman as qualified advice?

I hope that it is self-evident that you should not listen to the advice of those who have neither the experience nor qualifications or have not trodden on the path you have taken the decision to walk.

Take your advice from successful people. You will be able to leverage their mistakes and errors, making your path to success that little bit easier. As I alluded to before, my mentors and advisors have been some of the world's highest achievers and greatest speakers. On reflection, it was not the advice of my friends when I was growing up or co-workers who enabled me to have the confidence to make the decisions I did. The influence of those mentors and a small group of like-minded people resulted in me reaching my short- and medium-term goals.

Discipline is and has been the central tenet of my personal and professional development, and it is now part of my personal philosophy. I have always had a certain ability for self-control and self-discipline, but that was enhanced and then cemented during my years serving in the British Army. Joining the Forces at age sixteen helped me to structure my life and thought processes. (This was subconscious; sixteen-year-old Nathan had no idea this was happening.)

You may have a vision of that scary sergeant major screaming drill orders on the parade square, and you would not be too far wrong. But the British Army has had literally hundreds of years honing the way it instills discipline to make sure that British soldiers are among the finest in the world. Those early disciplines I learned during my twelve-week basic training at Army Training Regiment Bassingbourn included practicing a good daily hygiene routine, making your bed, structuring your day, identifying short- and medium-term goals, and working as part of a team.

Working as a team is not to be underestimated; it means constantly working to ensure that relationships are aligned, productive, and selfless. This list could go on and on, but these disciplines allowed me to promote ahead of my peers and make the move from soldier to a commissioned officer, allowing me to develop what I now realise is my real passion, leadership and the development of organisations and others.

I practiced my leadership and development skills, both formally through academia and professionally both in the UK and overseas, during peacetime and conflict. I have led hundreds of soldiers and officers and been part of critical international relationship negotiations with the UK's NATO allies. My role in NATO was to find solutions to problems; the business of war is costly in more ways than financial, and each one of the twenty-five individual member nations had a different tolerance to what they and their domestic population would find acceptable.

Under pressure, it is a natural human tendency to revert to the most basic and primitive responses to pressure, fight, or flight. I credit my ability to keep my head and clear mind under pressure with the basic disciplines I learned when I was sixteen at the Army Training Regiment (ATR) Bassingbourn, a truly wonderful and life-shaping experience.

On my journey, there have been two principal teachers whom I paid particular attention to, and they guided me, as they will guide you to your own success. The first is success itself; the second teacher is failure.

Ask yourself, "What is it that we learn from success?"

It is fantastic to succeed. It feels great. You become popular, liked, and respected. You ride the crest of a wave. You're on a high, and it confirms that your choices and decisions were correct.

But what did you learn? I would argue you learn nothing other than to continue with the same methodology for that success.

"Is that so bad?" you may ask.

Why shouldn't you do the same as you have done before to achieve success? That is because nothing in the universe is static. Humanity itself is in a state of constant evolution. It is innate to strive for growth, expansion, and innovation, and relatively speaking, if you are static, you are in effect going backward because you are surrounded by others who are striving forward, are motivated, and will not relent until they achieve their goals.

This is not to say that the pursuit of your goals is overtly an adversarial pursuit, but it does mean that if you are not the architect of your own success plan, you will be a piece in someone else's. Think about that.

Failure, on the other hand, feels horrible and is the antithesis of success. So why should you embrace such unpleasant results and the associated emotions? It's because failure is your greatest teacher and you have so much to learn from its lessons. Don't worry. The failure doesn't necessarily have to be yours; the smartest amongst you will learn from other people's failures, which is by far the most efficient and cost-effective way, to reap unimaginable value and reward at absolutely no cost to you. I can't wait to get into this bit, but we must piece this puzzle together sequentially, so you will have to wait until chapter 4 to learn the power of routine discipline.

I have written this book to be universally applicable to almost all situations, desires, and goals, and this is possible because the same traits for business success are the same for success on the sports field. In my own personal development over the past fifteen years and in research for this book, I found that the more I studied people and their journeys to success, the more apparent it became that there are universal and fundamental principles that underpin anybody's path to their personally defined success. I make use of anecdotes and metaphors because they are more easily relatable, and after all, who doesn't like a little story?

The anecdotes are also for you to apply to your own situation and your own plan because there is little point in me offering you a fixed path and step-by-step guide to follow. First, because I couldn't since I don't know you. And second, because this book is supposed to be ubiquitous to all areas of achievement, not just for those aspiring to climb the corporate ladder. It is as useful to someone who wants to be the best salesman in their department as it is to an athlete hoping to become a sporting champion or someone who desires to become a billionaire.

What this book will deliver for you is a widening of your awareness and that there is an absolute and essential requirement to educate yourself. It doesn't necessarily mean going to college or university, but it does mean educating yourself in the skills, knowledge, and experience required to succeed in your chosen area.

Let's look at sales to illustrate the point. If you wanted to achieve the best sales results in your department, then some innovative thinking could mean that understanding human psychology would be an excellent place to start. Strange, you might think, but I don't think so.

I would advocate studying human psychology because you will interact with people, no matter what you are trying to achieve. It's a core skill that you will need to master if you want to advance and go further in any chosen area of expertise. Professor Albert Mehrabian is often misquoted in saying that 93 percent of communication is nonverbal, but to get closer to the truth of this assertion, the good professor actually meant that of that 93 per cent, 55 per cent was attributed to body language, and 38 per cent was voice and tone.

This is fairly important stuff because it says to me that, to get on well with others or to interpret how others may be perceiving you, you should really be developing your emotional intelligence, picking up on other people's emotions, feelings, and attitudes. So with this in mind, let's go back to the salesperson. It should be obvious that in a sales scenario, people rely on the positive interaction with each other, buyers get what they want, agents earn commissions, and sellers hopefully get profits. It could mean taking a course in learning how to manage your time better. The better able you are at managing your time, the more potential clients you will be able to see, therefore increasing the chances of potential sales and so increasing the commissions you can earn.

What about using books or taking a course in public speaking? Have you ever seen a TED talk? If not, I highly recommend them. TED talks are hosted by the most intriguing presenters who speak with passion and excitement about their area of expertise. I have often found myself inspired to learn a little more about a seemingly random topic after hearing a confident and engaging speaker.

Our salesperson, armed with the confidence to talk to potential buyers, engaging them, enthusing them, and selling them their dream, will cover the costs of their public speaking course after their first sale. And the great news is that you only have to pay for that course or book once, but you get recurrent benefits from the lessons you have learned over and over again.

So there you go, with your confidence boosted, you understand your target audience. Now watch those sales roll in. This toolkit of disciplines, mindset, and a new understanding is all in support of helping you, and it really doesn't matter what you do because these skills are widely transferable.

What if you desired to be the best chef in the world? There are hundreds of examples of fine dining chefs around the world, and I would argue you must have complete mastery of the basic ingredients that go into not only your signature dish but every dish you produce. So how does a chef take themselves from being good or proficient to being the best, that standout exemplar who inspires the next generation and commands the respect of their peers?

Have you considered going to the gym more often to become physically fitter? Any chef from the head chef to the chef de partie will tell you that working in a hot kitchen is physically demanding, and I am an advocate of the "strong body equals a strong mind" philosophy. So our chef must be able to take the heat and not be drained by the exhausting work and pressure to deliver in a hot kitchen.

Let's not overlook the elevated position of leadership that a head chef occupies. You must be mentally strong in order to lead a team and maintain the highest standards of your restaurant and reputation. While most head chefs have obtained their position on their culinary skills, the role is a position of leadership, so I would think it prudent to undertake some leadership and management training to get those emotional intelligence skills up to scratch.

This newfound mental and physical strength will increase the head chef's performance and better equip them to lead and run a successful and efficient kitchen. This advantage will lead the aspiring chef down an easier path for culinary creativity, as well as the foundation for excellence in their field. Say hello to that Michelin star!

My personal favourite: what about the young, prospective millionaire? You wouldn't believe how long I spent as a kid wishing I were rich. I didn't really know what it meant to be rich, how to define rich, or how to be rich; nor did I realise that riches or wealth is a by-product of doing something else well. Some will think it's shallow; others will say that money will not make you happy. A few will make all manner of assumptions and judgments, but it's a goal and a target that has kept me motivated for over thirty years.

It began as my motivation and is now a means of keeping score. It has been a key performance indicator to measure my results and a target for my discipline. It has given me the focus and drive that has enabled me to do the most amazing things, meet the most interesting people, and, I hope, going forward, allow me to be even more generous and charitable than I ever thought possible.

Prospective millionaires amongst you are bursting with great ideas, all certain to make you wealthy beyond your wildest dreams. You're not able to sleep or contain your excitement at the future and vision you have painted for yourself. You can feel, smell, and taste the success, cars, and holidays, but there is one problem. They don't know where to start.

From experience, I have learned that in the pursuit of success in your chosen field, the one common goal I can identify is self-mastery. That requires investment in yourself, and this all begins at a decision point, the point in your life when you say, "Enough is enough. My time has come."

The way to read this book is for you to read small, bite-sized chunks and then put it down. Yes, put it down and think about what these lessons and messages mean to you or what you can apply to your future plans. As you turn your final page, what I hope to leave you with is a sense of direction, a roadmap for how you will execute your plan, to know how to make that most important first step and to start you on the path for personal excellence.

This book should be the most highlighted book in your collection. (Yes, you should have a collection.) Make notes on the side of the pages, along with the front and the back, as these will form part of your working plan for success. I have taken the liberty of emboldening some of the text for you. This is something that you really should take time to understand. If you don't, then read the sentence again before you move forward. All I ask is that you just give the book a chance and believe in your own ability to surpass any goal you ever thought possible.

I wrote this book because I decided to share my experiences, decisions, and motivations. This book would contribute to the existing body of work that has helped on my personal development journey and can help others on theirs. In this book, I want to deliver some clarity on the path you want to take, to give you the confidence to take that decision to move forward, and to be a better version of yourself today than you were yesterday but not as good as you will be tomorrow.

CHAPTER 1

You Are Your Most Valuable Commodity

The greatest form of mastery is mastery over one's self.
—Leonardo da Vinci

In reading the lives of great men, I found that the first victory they won was over themselves, self-discipline with all of them came first.
—Harry S. Truman

In the world of investing, analysts pore over hundreds of data points in order to gain a small insight to give them an edge over their competitors. The reason being is that a single extra piece of information or new insight can reap a company or individual millions of dollars in profits. Formula One racing teams adopt a similar philosophy: they invest hundreds of millions of dollars to gain a fraction of a second's advantage, which is the difference between winning and losing. This, in turn, relates to the quantity of prize money and the advertising revenue a team can generate from that same fraction of a second.

This same investment approach will become the method for your own development. You have entered the world of investment, and you are about to make the greatest investment you will ever make: the investment in yourself.

Take a look around yourself, literally and figuratively. Consider your immediate vicinity, your friends, and the world in which you wish to succeed. The people you see are both your competition and your allies, and it is your job to figure out which is which. You are faced with decisions every day that you need to make just to keep pace with everybody else. To stay one step ahead or at least take one more step toward your goal, you will have to make better, smarter decisions.

Consider every other person, friend or foe, as either a barrier or facilitator to you achieving your goals. With this in mind, we can consider that the best investment you could make is not necessarily a monetary investment or guidance from a guru; rather it's the time and energy you dedicate to taking care of your interests. If you don't, who will? Has a life planner approached you and mapped out your life for you? Have you had people rushing to help you achieve your goals and dreams?

I bet I know the answer to those questions. How much time in the past week, month, or even year have you dedicated to your own personal development? You need to answer this question, and this is a key moment where you should put down the book. Go on. Put the kettle on, and just make a note on what you have done for yourself in the past month and year that was solely for your own development. Be honest with yourself.

Ok, welcome back. Before I ask how you answered the question, I just want to highlight that at no point did I use the phrase *time management*. Why? Because you cannot do that. Unless you have the abilities of a higher power and can manipulate time itself, then the best you can do is to manage what you do with the time you have. It's not how many hours in the day you have; it's what you put into the hours you have that counts. This is about you, in case you hadn't realised that.

Now, back to my question. How much time have you set aside for yourself in the past month and year that was solely for your own development? For those most disciplined of individuals, excluding those in full- or part-time education, it could be as much as one hour per day! To others, that may seem like a pipe dream. But what does one hour per day really look like, and is it really achievable in the real world when we have to consider our personal morning routines? Let's break down a day's work for the average employee:

07:00   Wake up and put the kettle on.

07:30	Shower and perform any other morning hygiene routine. (If you have children, then you also have to get them ready for school.)
08:00	Eat breakfast .
08:30	Leave for work and/or the school run.
09:00–17:00	Work.
17:30	Come home.
18:00	Eat dinner (which is interchangeable with going to the gym).
19:00	Work out at the gym (which is interchangeable with dinner and perhaps not even every day).
20:00	Socialisation/your time
21:00–22:00	Personal development

This is an example of a generic routine, which is just a vehicle for me to demonstrate how someone can add five hours of personal development in a working week without a negative impact on a social life.

You could easily double this for short periods if you replace socialisation and your time with another hour of personal development. But how about using the socialisation time with friends for personal development? This would leverage your time much better, allowing you to build a network in the interests you have while interacting with like-minded people.

After all, this is effectively what a university is: it's a place where a group of like-minded individuals all want to learn a subject and are grouped into classes with other like-minded people. Often people studying in the same courses end up socialising with each other and talking about what they did that day. This practice lets you see how the other person interprets the day's lessons, and this added insight allows you to have a deeper view and understanding of the subject you are studying.

Even if you don't socialise with your fellow classmates and choose to socialise with people on other courses, this is not a bad thing. You benefit by broadening your horizon and getting further insight on something you may not have considered. What would be the outcome of a liberal arts student socialising with a sciences or engineering student? Each student represents an entirely different approach to problems, goals, and motivation, so I would argue that there is something to be gained from either side of that relationship.

Similarly, what about going to networking events or clubs associated with your development interest? Networking *is* personal development and an investment in yourself. We are fortunate enough today to have an endless supply of information in our pockets. You could easily take out your phone now and search, "Where can I do/play/meet [insert your chosen interest] near me?" You will be met with page after page of the location, community, and price of whatever you chose.

Network. We are social beings. You may get nervous; you may not like the idea of walking into a room of strangers. But I have to tell you: those strangers probably feel the same way as you do. If it really is too much for you to go and meet people, join an online social group and participate in forums. You can build you network that way, and it has the added benefit of not being geographically restricted. This may lead to a coffee with someone you click with, and then you're off.

It is no surprise or coincidence that the best networkers in the world are the same people who have risen to become captains of their own industry. So if you want to be at the top of yours, get networking. Leveraging networking events and learning from others are all hugely positive and necessary steps because you are less effective alone.

So back to maximising your development time. You could extend the amount of time you have in a day by waking up that little bit earlier. If you wake at 6:00 and continue with your routine up to having breakfast at 8:00, you could use the remaining ninety minutes of your morning on your development, be that reading, researching your area of interest or writing your development plan, or updating your CV. The list is endless. You can make this time even more effective by preparing some reading/ tasks the night before.

But magically, by waking only one hour earlier, you have gained ninety minutes extra in your day because you can apply a new discipline into your routine. During your personal development time the previous evening, you will have prepared your personal development material. You will have pre-filled the kettle and put a teabag in your cup (or coffee), and you will have prepared the material you need to research. This means when you wake up and while you're waiting for the kettle to boil, within fifteen minutes, you can have a cup of tea and devote this time to your personal development. That's the first hour accounted for; you create the next thirty minutes by replacing your original wake-up and tea drinking time with development. This is what discipline is.

Because you are not lying around in bed procrastinating, you have prepared better and set yourself up for success. Have you considered what an extra ninety minutes per day actually means over the course of a month or year? Let me show you. (I've even let you keep your weekends.)

90 minutes x 5 working days = 7 hours, 30 minutes per week
7 hours, 30 minutes x 4 weeks = 30 hours per month
30 hours per month x 12 months per year = 360 hours per year

Just what could you achieve with an extra 360 hours per year of personal development? You are limited only by your imagination, but you have to agree it's not a bad start. Malcolm Gladwell was a Canadian journalist who took the original works of Anders Ericsson, a Swedish psychologist, and said that you can become an expert in anything with 10,000 hours of practice.

I'm sure scores of PhD graduates have written whole theses on this, but in short, I just want to say it's nonsense. You can, and likely will, become an expert in anything with much less time invested than 10,000 hours, or 416 days (59 weeks) of solid practice, which is *years* of practice at 1 to 2 hours per day. I would say that your newfound 360 hours per year of development in your area of interest will give you above-average competence compared to your peers and an immeasurable amount of satisfaction and pleasure. So what are you waiting for?

I have used these practices over the past ten years in my own personal development, which have resulted in a set of disciplines that I live each day but can also enhance when I know I need to knuckle down and get something done. Having left high school in 1997 with no GCSEs[1] worth shouting about other than a B in English, I had long dreamt about having a degree. After all, everyone with a degree is really smart, aren't they?

So after years of deliberation, procrastination, and, I have to say, fear,

---

[1] General Certificate of Secondary Education, is a highschool qualification in England

I started a bachelor's degree in politics, philosophy, and economics via distance learning with the Open University. I decided to sacrifice my TV and leisure time for reading and study. (Much like now, I have replaced TV time for research and the writing of this book.)

But what I gained at the end of the course was more than just an honours degree. I learned valuable skills including skim reading, researching, understanding the credibility of the source of information, writing in different styles, presenting arguments, and, most critically, not so much time management but management of myself or, as I call it, self-management.

All of this was underpinned by discipline, the discipline in myself to ring-fence specific times for study and even a little extra study time when I had factored in holiday periods and the discipline of consistency. Jim Rohn says discipline isn't the easy option. It's a full-time activity, and the same discipline it takes to make your bed every day is the same discipline it takes to be a business success.

I couldn't agree more. I finished that degree, and ten years on, I completed a second honours degree in leadership and management, a post-graduate diploma in business, and finally a master's degree. I have the utmost respect for those who embark on any level of learning, especially as an adult. It's bloody difficult!

With this experience behind me, I can say with absolute conviction that I don't feel like I lost out or missed out on anything socially and that once I was in a rhythm of study, it was really no hardship at all. This is a real example of how the self-management techniques you have just learned can be put into practice, culminating in a real and successful end state, but that end state is not limited to academic qualifications. They could just as easily be vocational and practical goals.

Should you decide to, you could use these same techniques to improve an area you want to work on. It could be an hour each day researching anything that takes you one step closer to reaching your goals. I still don't spend any time watching TV. For me, there is always something to learn or research for the development of my business and for my continual journey down the path of personal development. Life is short, and we don't have time to waste. What are you going to do with that extra hour a day?

Are you going to use it to take one step closer to your goals? There are no excuses now. Back yourself. You can do it.

The best investments I have made in the last decade have all been in intellectual capital (education). I looked at my end states and where I wanted to be in twenty years and simply worked backward in a logical, step-by-step process. That thought experiment gave me a road map for me to hold myself to account as to how well I had performed that year in what I had set out to achieve, and you could do the same too. This process is called ends, ways, and means analysis, and I borrowed it from my time in the military. A core responsibility for me as a commissioned officer is to think strategically.

So with many of the processes I learned while in the army, I adapted them to fit my own personal development goals. Work with me through this following example and try to apply this method to your own goals. In military parlance, the *ends* are the strategic goals you want to achieve. Militarily, that may be to free a population under autocratic rule. For me, it was to gain a degree. So far so good. Now I had identified my goal.

I then needed to understand the *ways*, or how I was going to achieve my ends (goals). Militarily, it would be described as the methods, tactics, procedures, and practices that I would employ to give the greatest chance of success in achieving the predetermined ends (goals). Nowadays I would describe that as identifying the tools, resources, and disciplines I would need to get me to that elusive degree.

Back in 2012, I identified that I had time to spare, as I described previously. I also knew I would have to change some of my routines. No more documentaries and oddly start spending more time in cafés. Yes, I'll expand on this later.

So finally we come to the *means*. The army would say it's the resources required to achieve the ends, such as troops, weapons systems, money, political will, and time. For me, I needed to pay for the course. I was fortunate enough to have funding available from the army to help me pay for the tuition. I had found an institution that would allow me to do a degree without the need for A-levels.[2] I had all the hardware I needed to engage with the course: books, laptop, and the motivation to see the course

---

[2] A-levels are college qualifications that are usually required to gain a place at University

through to the end. So I had reached a decision point. There was nothing standing in my way. I just had to say yes.

Ends, ways, and means analysis of yourself and your goals is an excellent tool for investing in yourself because it allows you to create a vision, resource it, and plan the execution of it. It's the vision of your preferred self that is unconstrained by difficulty and obstacles that are present in our day-to-day lives. This is similar to the purity of thought that a child has, before the expectation of society and the influence of their close circle and social media have in their daily lives. To take that vision and breathe life into it by taking a step forward in small bite-sized chunks and not over committing too early as the goal might just appear too great. But before you know it, that goal way out on the horizon becomes a story to share with someone who is about to begin their own journey. Your story becomes somebody else's inspiration.

The beauty of this most basic of approaches is that it affords you the benefit of seeing into the future! Think of it this way. How many times have you said to yourself or heard others say, "If I'd have known then what I know now …" or "If I could go back and give myself some advice …"? Well, that's exactly what you are doing. You are setting out to do the very thing you want to do, planning how to do it and actually doing it. (Goodness, that's a lot of doing.)

As with all crystal balls, when you look into them, they are a little blurry, and you can't quite see with absolute clarity what is going to happen, and that's fine. What this vision gives you is enough for you to make a rough plan, a plan that when worked backward will show you what the first step is. It could be to buy a specific book. It could be this book! It's a plan that is vague enough for you to make adjustments along the journey and a plan that will ensure your vision becomes a reality. Those obstacles you identify aren't really obstacles at all. With the benefit of hindsight plus your plan, they become checkpoints for you to measure your success in stages. They are the things you will talk about. They are the things that give value to your goals. You should wish for more of them, not less. Just use your disciplines to become better.

So we now know that it's important to spend a little time looking after our own interests. Let's call it "minding your own business" from now on. You are your own business. You are your best asset, and now you are going to invest in that business. So you should welcome what is normally considered an unfriendly remark and consider it to be not only very good advice but your mantra every time you pause for thought and reflect on how much personal development you have done in the passing weeks or months. Mind your own business.

So far we have identified that no matter how rich you are or what colour or race you are, we all have the same twenty-four hours in a day. We have identified that we can't really manage time, but we can manage ourselves better and get more out of our twenty-four hours per day with effective self-management. So now we can ask, "Where do we invest that newly found spare capacity?"

Let's look at a couple examples, but remember, this isn't to be taken literally. You need to apply the thought process and have an open-enough mind to apply these examples to your own goals.

If you wanted to be the fastest ten-kilometre runner in your running club, what areas might you consider it wise for investing time and energy into? Your first response may be to train harder or more regularly, perhaps even using that extra ninety minutes we found in the morning during the self-management example discussed previously for more training.

I'd say that was sensible and would agree that you would see gains and improvement in your running time. Job done? Well, maybe not. You see, this is conventional thinking, so you can be sure that everybody else in your running club is probably thinking the same thing. You would perhaps buddy up with someone else in the club to do that extra training with, so your gains being relative to everyone else means the aggregate ten-kilometre running time across your whole club might come down, which is wonderful for your club, but your average position compared to your peers is unlikely to change.

Remember, your goal was not just to become a faster runner. It was to be the fastest runner in your club. We need to elevate our thinking and see what other marginal gains we can reach by researching everything about your running style and having running professionals analyse your gait analysis. What about researching the best or most suitable running trainers for your running style? Perhaps even complete a course in weight training to strengthen muscles and increase power and endurance in your legs? Wouldn't you agree that exploring these other areas will improve your running time?

I think it's reasonable to assume that if your running analysis has revealed that you are a little flat-footed and therefore would be better suited to use a specific type of running shoe, are you an over- or under pronator. Do you need a more flexible midsole? A change in your running shoe would translate into being more comfortable during your training sessions. This in addition to the extra strength training you have learned about and gained by introducing strength conditioning into your program means your legs would be stronger.

The culmination of this more granular analysis would culminate into being more relaxed when you are running, and halfway through your run, you would feel less fatigued because your muscles are stronger. By the time you crossed the finish line, you might be surprised that with only a little bit of investment in developing yourself, that has translated into you being a more accomplished runner. And you are well on your way to achieving your goal of being the fastest ten-kilometre runner in your club.

It is small and incremental gains that athletes in any sport seek to improve to end up with a performance package that is greater than the sum of its parts. No single exercise will deliver you to your goals and dreams. You must become a master of incremental improvement and monitor your losses and gains to make sure you are moving toward your goals.

Is business more your thing? For instance, say your goal was to give up paid employment and start your own coffee shop business. Coffee shops are really in vogue at the minute, and it's really easy to see why. They are great communal spaces where you can go to chill out or be inspired.

So armed with your vision of where you want to be, where do you think might be a good place to start with the extra time in the day you have made for yourself? I'd begin with a blank piece of paper and a pencil, ready to create my mind map. Mind mapping is an excellent tool for dumping information on a subject into a single visual plan.

For our coffee shop entrepreneur, the potential list of items that need to be considered could be massive, and there are whole books out there to give you a great head start, but that is not the aim of this book. So don't worry. I won't cover everything here.

Before you spend a penny, you must research, research, research. Use the internet and network with local small business communities. Find a mentor and complete the due diligence. Can you afford to give up work? What if the revenues are lower than your initial estimation? Where are you opening your shop? Is the footfall high enough? (Just how many people actually do walk past in a day?) Is there any local competition?

I don't think that any local café owner would be too happy that you are planning to open up in an area too close to them and potentially stealing sales. What about the type of blend you want to serve? A bitter blend or something more fruity? Or do you want a blend to reflect your personality or brand of your business? Have you considered the price point for each of the drinks on your menu? Who is your competition? Where are you going to get your stock? Is it ethically sourced? Are there any government grants available? Which accountants' firm will you use for filing your end-of-year tax returns? Do you know what kind of information you need to keep for your tax return, and will you employ staff? This list goes on and on.

But once this list has been considered, you will be forearmed with the information you need to maximize the chances of business success. You need this level of commitment for a chance of success, not to guarantee success. I would argue that start-ups fail early is because many an entrepreneur didn't do their research. But you're different. There's a lot to do in that one to two hours per day you have made for yourself, but remember, ninety minutes per day is 360 hours per year.

I think that, with 360 hours of research and preparation, anybody could start a successful coffee shop. Minding your own business pays dividends, literally and metaphorically, and will give you personal satisfaction, which translates into happiness and ultimately will lead you to achieving your goals.

These two examples serve as demonstrations of how you can take an idea and identify some, if not most, of the necessary steps to achieving your vision. This is an investment in yourself. You do this once, and you reap the rewards time and time again.

Consider the fringe benefits for the ten-kilometre runner. They have mastered their ability to manage themselves better and maximise the amount of time they can dedicate to training. They are fitter, healthier, and stronger, and they can apply these benefits to other aspects of their lives, including widening a social network and supporting and mentoring other runners. (Therefore, they become a pseudo teacher, experiencing all of the positive feelings that brings.) And finally, they are probably happier at work and more productive because of how good they feel.

Similarly, the coffee shop business owner has now become their own boss. They have also mastered themselves and maximised their outputs during the course of their working day, and now they can teach those skills to others. They have managed to employ some other staff and therefore give somebody else an opportunity to work and feel like a valued member of society. They have added to their local economy, and there is an increasing sense of community as the café has become a meeting place for others.

Twelve months later, that same owner has expanded and opened a second shop. They have employed more people, trained their original baristas in management to run the new shop, and are mentoring a young entrepreneur to take their first tentative steps into business. And all of this because they decided to invest in themselves. Wow, who would have thought the impact could be that broad?

The point here is whatever your chosen field, there will be an enormous amount of variables you should consider. All of which will take time to research even if you think you already know your subject. But once you have your plan and put it into practice, there is a community of people that will benefit from your success. In addition to this, countless others will benefit from your success, if not directly but indirectly, as you inspire someone else to pursue their dreams.

No matter what you decide in life or what field or activity you choose to embark on, there will be no better investment in that field than the continual personal and professional development you impose on yourself. Your investment decisions, such as your ability to manage yourself and get more out of your twenty-four hours each day, are totally transferable to any and every pursuit in life.

None of this investment is ever wasted. You are your most valuable commodity, so I hope you get the message of this chapter: invest in yourself. Learn to work harder on yourself. Then you do your job. Work full time at your job and part time on your future because in no time at all, your future will be upon you, and your job will be a distant memory. Jim Rohn says, "Work hard on your job you will make a living, work hard on yourself you will make a fortune."

CHAPTER 2

Distractions

Superman was wasting his time as a crime fighter [in Metropolis]! He would better serve the world if he had used his strength and speed to end world hunger, and advance our desire for clean energy.

—Miroslav Kohut

I think this quote is a great one for illustrating how we might become distracted. What this says to me is that we all have a certain skillset or ability that, if used effectively, can achieve the greatest things. The world's problem in this case was that Superman didn't realise what he was really was good at, and as a result, he was distracted by the minor and very local issues of fighting crime in Metropolis and his love interest with Lois Lane rather than using his amazing powers to have a deep and meaningful impact across the globe. Metropolis's gain was the world's loss! You can't allow yourself to become distracted from the path to achieving your goals.

The issue for most people (and I include an earlier version of myself in that sweeping statement) is they never discover what they're good at because they are distracted by minor short-term gratification or, even worse, don't believe they deserve all that their dreams present to them. There are no prizes for guessing what serves as a distraction today, but by way of a quick exercise, what do you think is a distraction to your focus and concentration? What does that distraction look like? Social media? TV? Can't resist that boxset that everyone in the office is talking about? Do you have a bit of fear of missing out (FOMO)? Domestic chores perhaps?

"I haven't got time to sit and read," I hear you say.

You have a huge pile of washing to do, ironing, and cleaning your home. After all, we are all house proud, are we not? Partners, sadly some people, are in very unproductive relationships where the mere suggestion of wanting to do something better for one's self would cause an argument. This book is not relationship guidance, but I will say if any of the above resonates with you, then this is the first major issue you need to attend to before moving any further into your personal development plan.

Family and friends? Goodness, surely we can rely on our family and friends to offer support in your newfound desire for personal development. Sadly, I have to tell you that might not always be the case, and again if the cap fits, it's not necessarily a fault of those family members or friends that they have a generally unsupportive attitude toward your vision. They may not be equipped with your vision nor have any of the necessary experience to relate to what you are talking about.

Imagine saying to your friends that you want to create a reusable rocket so you can make it possible to commercialise space travel and eventually colonise Mars. Yeah sure! They would ask you if you are on any medication for that, but this is exactly the vision for Elon Musk, serial entrepreneur, PayPal cofounder, and CEO of Tesla and Space X. Imagine if he listed to his doubters, old friends who hadn't gone into the tech industry.

Imagine them saying, "Hey, Elon, forget that internet banking stuff or starting your own company. Nah, it won't work. Come work in retail with us."

I would argue the world would be a much worse place. This just serves to illustrate that our friends and family may have inherent fears about failure and cannot possibly perceive a way to succeed. In their minds, success is reserved for people who went to better schools or university or had a leg-up from a family friend.

For parents reading this book, how about your children? Are they or have they become a distraction or an excuse for you not to pursue your goals? I am well aware of the controversy this statement may cause, but I'm trying to illustrate that you mustn't make excuses. There are thousands of successful single-parent families out there, all with parents who are doing exactly what they wanted to do, and having children is not a reason to avoid pursuing your own goals.

I know it's tough as a parent. You have to make sure your children are looked after, prepare packed lunches for school, get clothes washed and ironed, and take them to after-school clubs. It's essentially a full-time job with no pay. All of a sudden, the time schedule I illustrated previously gets more and more marginalised to a point where it might feel that you need to extend your day out to about twenty-six hours to fit everything in.

But how about setting this example to your kids that despite all of the things you have to do every day for others, you make time for the things you want to do for yourself? What a great example and set of habits to pass on to your children. Your challenge (as was and is still mine) is to balance the needs and demands of all of these distractions and to make sure you commit the time necessary for your own personal development. This will be difficult, but you have to get over it if you are to seize the future you envisioned for yourself and ultimately deserve.

While writing my master's thesis, it occurred to me that in the quiet comfort of my office in my own home, everything and anything distracted me. Frustrated by this, I stumbled on my perfect environment for personal development by a moment of enlightenment as I sat sipping a frothy coffee made by my favourite barista chain. I realised how comfortable I was in the environment. Despite the gentle hum of conversation, the steaming of milk by the ridiculously large coffee machine that only spits out a shot of espresso, and the temptation of cakes and pastry, I found it very easy to focus on my work.

In later professional development, I discovered that this was called a personal learning environment, which is essentially a space where all of your immediate needs are satisfied and your mind is calm enough to allow you to focus on a specific task for an unlimited amount of time. With this new understanding, I have simply leveraged that knowledge over and over again to eliminate distraction and to get things done. I decided to solve my distraction problems and create a personal development environment. I renamed the concept to development rather than learning, but that's my preference. You need to discover the magic of a Personal Development Environment because this will solve most, if not all, of your distraction problems. Your PDE may reveal itself to be in the most unusual of places. Allow me to explain why knowing what distracts you, where your quiet space is, and exactly how you respond best to new information benefits you.

How Learning Was Used and How It Developed

When you think of a learning environment, what do you think of? What do you see in your mind's eye? A school, right? Traditionally we consider the learning environment to be a specific and purpose-built location with a handful of teachers among a sea of students, unless of course you went to a more privileged school where the ratios were much more conducive to focused learning. Learning is considered to be a full-time activity with active repetition, copying text from blackboards, or poring over texts for hours on end with the vain hope that you pass an exam, which seems to be looming ever closer with every passing day.

And let's not forget the dreaded homework that you have let pile up because having one night off to relax doesn't seem that bad … until you realise that the exam or submission deadline is tomorrow at midnight. This antiquated description has been consigned to the past, and thankfully times have now changed.

As we have progressed through the Iron Ages, Middle Ages, and Industrial Revolution, these periods were dependent on a robust and physical skillset to develop the technologies of the day. Labouring on a farm; working materials such as metal, hides, or leather; baking; and candlestick making were all functions and activities that powered local and eventually national economies, even to this day. These skillsets are synonymous with lifelong careers with families rooted in similar trades. It would be very common for a son or daughter to follow a family tradition of work without consideration of moving into something different. Fast-forward to present day (from the 1970s), the advent of the computer catapulted the progress of industry to what I will call the Internet/Electronic Age.

In this new age, careers in single organisations are uncommon, and work is much more transient and spread across greater distances. Employment for millennials is more likely to be short, more specialised, and shifting from opportunity to opportunity, and here we are at the zenith of the development of the employment model as the gig economy is in full swing. Employers are equally as choosy about those they employ, electing to poach or headhunt high-value employees or tender to an agency based on the speedy accessibility of potential employees with the right skillset for a specific period of time to enable the company to grow and develop so it can forge a competitive advantage in its own market until that market changes. This is why people are made redundant! The process isn't any different from before. It's just speeded up due to computerisation and robotisation of industry. It's worth giving you a bit of context before we go any further.

Adult versus Child Learning

We have all seen or heard a bilingual child speak, and we stand there in wonder at how a young boy or girl can switch between languages with unbelievable ease. I have sat in and stared in wonder at this, with particular reference to a couple friends of mine who were born Romania, lived and worked in Belgium and Italy, and now reside in England. Their two children speak all of the aforementioned nations' languages!

When I was serving in the army, a new piece of policy issued required all majors (my retirement rank) who wanted to promote to lieutenant colonel had to speak a second language to a reasonable level. We had the luxury of choosing from French, German, Spanish, Russian, and Arabic. Having done high school French twenty-five years earlier, I thought I could trawl the few remaining dusty brain cells I had left to be able to attend the course and scrape a pass.

I can tell you that I might as well have chosen Russian because I had absolutely no recollection of my prior learning beyond counting to ten and an annoying chorus of a French children's song my French tutor insisted on teaching us. Twenty-five years later, I sat with a troop of my fellow comrades, trying desperately to learn enough to pass this course, in the vain hope that we would have a slight competitive advantage on the next promotion board.

After two weeks of intense study, your author, through luck, fate, or alchemy, managed to pass his level-two French course. Tres bien, Monsieur John! I shudder now at the thought of learning a new language with all of my ingrained adult biases, but why is this?

After a little observation and thought, I think the main difference is that for an adult, it is the decision or choice to learn rather than the need or expectation to learn. That makes all of the difference. That child with multilingual parents is under no pressure to learn two to four different ways to say "hello" if they want to communicate with their mother or father. For an adult in the Western world, there really isn't a need to learn to speak another language as the vast majority of the world now speaks English, so we have become linguistically lazy.

The pace and rate that you understand and can assimilate information is another critical factor and mustn't be overlooked. It's different for different people, and this presents itself most obviously in the junior and high school environment because after this, learning becomes more of a choice. Therefore young adults are more likely to want to learn.

From experience, I can safely say that I was absolutely not ready to learn during my teenage years. I wouldn't go as far as to say I was disruptive, but I certainly wasn't engaged or enthused by my teachers. Perhaps this was due to the pace of learning, and once I fell behind, those government targets and statistics would wait for no child!

With my 20/20 hindsight, it's the sole purpose for a teacher to enthuse and engage with their pupils and make sure they can find a way to pass on knowledge. My schoolteachers failed, a bold statement I know, but I believe it to be true. Fortunately I found a love for learning later on in life, and the rest is history. The point here is that adults can regulate the speed in which they learn. Once you have decided to learn something new, something that piques your interest, you make time for learning.

This self-regulated learning means that all the content will sink in, thus enriching your learning experience. Since its launch in 1969, 1.94 million people have enrolled and studied with the Open University and achieved their learning goals. 76 per cent of students are in full- or part-time work! And nearly a quarter of all graduates are from the most deprived areas in the UK.

This is great news for you. There is a whole community of people out there who will support you in your own personal development journey, individuals reading books like this who know what you are going through because they share the same challenges. What's stopping you? What excuse do you have not to?

How Do You Learn?

"Work on the roots and don't focus on the fruits." This is a lovely little quote but also a very powerful illustration of the difference between those who are fantastically successful in achieving the goals they have set themselves and those who simply don't. Looking back at the chef, salesperson, and other examples I used in chapter 1, the methods for achieving excellence was the focus on the minutiae, the details, and the foundation. It wasn't a focus on the fruits, the outcomes, and the successes. No, these were the original visions that fed your decision to fulfil your wants and desires. So how do we make this learning thing easier?

We have looked at why we should learn. We have considered where we should learn, so now we should consider how we should learn. Why? Because it is possibly the most crucial of all three considerations because understanding this is your key to absorbing massive quantities of information, more than you ever thought possible. Have you ever considered what kind of learner you are? It's not really an everyday question that we ask ourselves, so I wouldn't be surprised at your answer.

Let's bring this to life. You arrive home, having been shopping at your local flat-pack furniture store. You have filled the back of the car with boxes of what will become a new set of drawers in your lounge. Now all that's stopping you from filling this space is a cup of tea and a single hexagon key. Do you prefer reading instruction manuals first before you get stuck into assembling that piece of flat-pack furniture? Would you prefer someone show you how to do something first and then have you copy them afterwards?

Well, some clever souls have taken it upon themselves to study different kinds of learning preferences. I'm not going to delve into this in detail, but what I will say is that you probably fall into one of five learning categories:

- **Visual Learner:** You prefer to see diagrams and pictures to help you understand what you are being taught. You perhaps make notes in shapes, diagrams, and different colours. This is where I sit, so you can see that listening to an unenthusiastic teacher probably won't afford you the best opportunity to be your best!

- **Audio Learner:** You like to listen to instructions, take notes, and possibly ask questions to help you understand. You like structure, and your notes are likely to be neat and tidy.
- **Read/Write Learner:** You like to read text. You really like libraries and can sit for hours poring over books or instructions. Your note-taking is probably the neatest of all learners, in nice, legible lines.
- **Kinsaesthetic Learner:** This is a tactile learning style. You like hands-on learning and are most suited, but not limited, to hands-on work. You are probably not a fan of note-taking and may find that this preferred learning style is linked to visual learning. A fair amount of anecdotal evidence shows that young teens who get in trouble in school with behaviours that escalate into minor and even major crime are in fact kinaesthetic learners, but the Western education system doesn't cater for their needs. If these youngsters do make it through the school system, they will often choose the world of work or an apprenticeship as opposed to college and university.

There is a fifth style called **multi-modal**, but this really refers to someone who is able to learn via any of the styles above. This is an interesting arena for you to explore and ultimately learn more about yourself. Just Google "VARK" for more information.

There are probably a few readers who are looking at the list above and thinking, "Well, I think I'm a bit of both." That's entirely fine. You do not have to fit neatly into the boxes that society says you should. You are free to understand who you are. I myself am very visual, so I find that when I am learning from an audiobook, reading text, or being shown something, my notes are in blocks and shapes, and I use different colours to help me make sense of the information, as this is how I distil information I can't understand easily. This insight revolutionised my appetite for learning, and I have never looked back.

I hope you see the value in the context and the benefit of understanding distractions. Not knowing your learning style is the ultimate distraction for you. As we covered in chapter 1, you are your most valuable commodity, so you should take care to grow and develop your skills and experiences, making yourself better and more valuable to you and those around you. Remember, work on your roots. Don't focus on the fruits.

Personal Development Environment (PDE)

We are going to look at what this is, where it is, and why it's important to you. Finding my PDE was a key part of my own personal development journey, as it enabled so many of the important foundations we have already discussed.

I am now able to significantly minimise the distractions to the goals I had set for myself and, in extremis, such as a business deadline or writing target date, eliminate the distractions completely. You really should be giving yourself the best opportunity to stay focused. Don't cheat yourself. It is a key discipline to continue good habits that will support your journey to success. Your PDE is your secret weapon to supercharge your productivity, no matter what you are doing, be that studying for coursework, planning a business, or taking just a bit of time for you to reflect on your progress.

It's a space that enables you to take control of your development. You are surrounded by distractions, so it is your business to make sure you control the few things you really can, one of which is the environment you are in. I mentioned previously a few common distractions we face today, such as social media, TV, domestic chores, home, partners, family, friends, children, and work commitments. Let's look at what you might be doing in order to allow yourself to be distracted.

How often do you check your social media profiles during the day? A quick check every twenty minutes or possibly more? That's fine as a cursory check, but this is the absolute archenemy of concentration needed for you to achieve your goals. Most phones today will break down your usage into the apps you are looking at and how much screen time you are viewing each day.

I don't consider myself to be a prolific uploader of content or gamer, so I don't think I spend that much time on my phone beyond that cursory check or quick email. My phone usage on average is two hours and thirty minutes per day over a seven-day period. I also average 93 pickups per day (mostly on a Wednesday for some reason), and when I look at the apps I use, mostly it is productivity apps like my Outlook app and Apple

Messenger, which seems about right as I do use my phone as a computer when I'm away from the office. The other apps that feature highly are my newspaper apps and then YouTube. Social media is not even in my top ten.

However, I do concede that for some people, they derive their living from a heavy online and proactive presence. There are people out there making handsome profits off social media channels, and I salute you, but I guarantee there is a lot of hard work going on in the background to make those channels a success.

Think of it this way. Those social media influencers are working on their roots every day, and you don't see it at all. What you see and watch are the fruits, their content and their glamorous lives. So unless your goal has a social media requirement, your constant checking in is probably costing you your dreams. For me, two hours and thirty minutes per day, what does that look like over a year? The answer: Over nine hundred hours per year. What could I learn or do with that much extra time? This is guilt-free, as most of those hours are used for productivity and not leisure.

Today and now more than ever, we are unconsciously influenced by society, companies, and their marketing departments, government, and the ubiquitous social media channels. For some, checking your phone while having a conversation with another person or group of people would be considered very rude, but now we are more accepting in having conversations while looking at our phones, checking texts, surfing the internet, or playing games.

Why is this? Speed and gratification. In the early 2000s, dial-up internet was all that was available. Speeds were measured in kilobytes per second, but as the general internet user hadn't experienced anything other than this, it was accepted that it could take five to ten minutes for a page to load! As time progressed, companies competed for your business by offering quicker internet speeds and more storage.

What am I getting at? Time has always been sold as the most valuable commodity, and companies know they can sell you something that promises to give you more time. A quicker internet connection saves you time and stops you from becoming frustrated. How many times have you cursed at your laptop for freezing or not loading quickly enough? If businesses know this and invest millions of dollars into saving you a few seconds on your ability to download a movie or play an online game, then perhaps it's about time you started to value your time a little more highly.

The question for you is how much unproductive time do you spend on your phones, and what do you think you could do to make a positive change for yourself? This isn't a judgment, and I'm not saying you should go totally monk or nun, but give yourself a chance. Moderate your use and spend a little time on your development.

Barriers to Development

Educating yourself is a time-intensive process and can even feel a bit antisocial. It does require the investment of not only your time, but additional energy in doing what you are supposed to be learning about. The converse here is sadly that it is easier for you not to learn; it is easier for you to start that boxset that everyone in the office is raving about. It is easier for you to check your social media, but none of those activities will help deliver your goals.

I know that when you take that decision to make a change, be that a new diet, a change of routine, or a new college course, the start is great. You feel great because you have taken that step to learn something new. You tell your friends, and they coo and tell you "well done."

But then as life goes on and you start to fall behind on the gossip around the latest TV show, this starts to weigh heavily on your motivation to carry on. Sustaining the level of self-discipline and effort required to see your course or project through to the finish is an entirely different matter, and it will separate you from success or not. (I don't like to use the words *fail* or *failure*, as I believe there are lessons in everything we do if you look for them.)

I asked you if you knew the cost of the quick check of your phone throughout the day earlier, so let's take a look. Social media and its role in distracting you is devilishly simple. That momentary check of an update, email, or YouTube link will grow into thirty minutes of internet surfing before you know it.

So how might this affect you? Well, think back to the ninety minutes you gained earlier by waking up earlier. That quick check of your profile has meant that waking up thirty minutes earlier has taken a third of your daily allocated study time, time you set aside for yourself. Imagine that, a third of your time taken up by just checking your phone when you could be researching how to get your business idea off the ground.

Domestic chores and home life are in a way worse than checking your phone and social media because these are necessities. Nobody wants to live in an untidy or smelly house, so we routinely attack those boring chores either on the weekends or a little bit every day. My personal method is to clean up after myself daily and do a thorough clean at the weekends. But outsourcing this could be a real genius idea. You could pay a professional cleaner and use your old cleaning time toward achieving your goals.

It's really important to not then use this time to catch up on boxsets because if you don't use this time effectively, then all you have done is increase your expenditure each month. Yes, there are readers out there who will argue that you have also increased your quality of life, and I do not doubt or argue that point, but this book is about personal development, which will eventually see you with the best work/life balance possible because you love your work and life has been enhanced by the work that you now love!

That small investment in a cleaner or someone to iron your clothes could give you your goals sooner than you think, and if that is business success, then that same investment would be paying for itself. I'm not going to; nor could I prescribe what is best here. That is something that has to fit your routine and your long-term goals, but as with social media, an untidy environment is a distraction, and you will not be able to think clearly. What is it they say? Tidy desk, tidy mind? For this reason, it's probably easier to ring-fence study time rather than try to control all of the other factors affecting your study, perhaps even removing yourself from the environment. Do it once or twice, and it will become a pleasant habit.

Partners, family, and friends, this is an area of distraction where you need to tread carefully. Aspiration, ambition, and drive are usually individual and lone journeys taken when an individual is ready to move forward. "When the student is ready, the teacher will appear." I have heard this phrase so many times over the years and never really understood its meaning until I was ready. It was amazing how many people presented themselves as an inspiration to me or had something to teach, but not literally of course. It's more that I was open to and able to see that I could learn something from someone else or that I had the confidence to go and ask for help, which I have discovered is a rare ability.

When I think of it, I don't often see people outright ask for help. In my experience, it presents itself in a variety of other ways like misbehaviour, stress, frustration, and other not very pleasant experiences. I find it easy to ask for help, and this is because I'm not the best at anything. Nor do I have a monopoly on all of the good ideas. So I have to ask, and in so doing, I have made some fantastic friends. I got some priceless ideas and moved forward toward my own goals at a much quicker pace than if I hadn't asked. It's food for thought.

This newfound inspiration is difficult to sell or convince partners, family, and friends. They may be sceptical of your ideas, they have totally different life experiences than you, and they may not be inspired or driven to achieve the same goals you do. So don't expect them to be fully on board or supportive. This means when you ring-fence time for your personal development, this can appear to be a selfish thing to do from their perspective. This isn't a bad judgment on them. While they probably do want to see you do well, they are also wedded to their comfort zone, and you are part of that. So your radical ideas force a departure from the norm.

From my experience, you will find that unless your family and friends have done something similar, they will unlikely be able to empathise with you, which may leave you lonely and isolated. This is natural. Humans are social beings and share life and experiences. Be prepared for support in the beginning (hopefully continuing throughout) and criticism as you study.

One remedy for this that I have found is first and foremost you will expand your network and friends groups naturally as you develop your new skills and abilities, but the best thing you can do is find a mentor, someone who has been there and done that. Not only will they enhance all of your current learning, they will be able to guide you around the pitfalls and mistakes they made along the way.

I remember this quite vividly in my own development into business and my first business deal after leaving the army where my mentor constantly used to tell me to focus on generating sales. This was difficult for me because I am not a natural salesman at all. In fact, the thought of being a salesman makes my skin crawl, but he wasn't asking me to be a salesman. He was asking me to focus on sales. This shift in mindset totally altered my approach to business and gave me a new toolset to approach any business transaction I became involved in thereafter.

This doesn't ever stop. I am not a complete business genius and don't expect I ever will be. Business isn't a zero-sum game in the same way as winning the 100-metre Olympic Gold, but I will constantly develop myself to make sure I can keep pace and make intelligent decisions. You must do the same, and if your goal is to be number one in something, then so be it. Use these tools and methods in the cultivation of your roots and keep your eyes on the prize.

CHAPTER 3

Belief

To believe in something and not live it is dishonest.
—Mahatma Gandhi

This is such an important chapter because it's not a matter of getting this right or working through steps to arrive at the belief destination. There is no compromise here. The equation is simple: if you believe in yourself, you will succeed. If you're not honest with yourself and have doubts, you won't.

Belief is a peculiar concept with its etymology found in Middle English origin. It derives ownership of property (in this case, your intellectual property). It's useful to understand this because when you find you have difficulty in explaining or selling your idea to friends, family, or colleagues, that may be because of two possible reasons:

1. You just didn't explain it well enough.
2. More likely, your belief is entirely personal.

Welcome to the isolation of a visionary on their road to success. Synonyms of belief include individual, eccentric, bizarre, extraordinary, or unique. So if you find that you are described in this way, that is a huge compliment and a signal that you are doing something right, and if you're reading this book, you likely want to be anything but ordinary.

Oprah Winfrey once said, "You don't manifest what you want; you manifest what you believe." This same understanding was supported by

Jim Rohn, who said, "You become what you believe." Or how about Barack Obama, whose closest friends assert that his ascent to the presidency was underpinned by one single key driver, his own preternatural self-assurance and a seemingly unshakeable belief in his own rhetorical and intellectual gifts. Can you think of a better speaker than Barack Obama?

Look around you and you will see the product of an individual's belief in everyday life. A little over a hundred years ago, aeroplanes didn't exist, but that didn't stop the Wright brothers in their pursuit to make humans fly. How many people do you suppose said to them between 1900 and 1903, as they trialled multiple iterations of aircraft, "This will not work. You are crazy," or a million other reasons why not to continue with their pursuit of powered flight.

I, for one, am glad they did push on, and they were resolute in achieving the goals they set themselves. I know what you're thinking, "But that was over a hundred years ago. Nothing like that happens anymore." Tell that to the late Steve Jobs, who not only invented a whole subcategory of personal electronic devices (smartphones and tablets) but also created from nothing a platform for which exponential improvements can be made in just about every field in human existence.

I'm talking about apps. You have heard the phrase, "There's an app for that." Well, just think for a moment. Can you think of a topic/field/hobby where there isn't an app available for it? No matter what brand of computer or smartphone hardware, I guarantee it has been influenced directly or indirectly by Steve Jobs and his self-belief and vision for an interconnected future. He once said, "People don't know what they want until you show it to them." Now that's belief.

For you and I as onlookers to these examples and what we see every day, that same belief doesn't seem the same, does it? It somehow seems easier for other people, I know. I assure you that nobody questions my belief more than me. That same seed of doubt sewn at some point in my life seems to reappear overnight, like the annoying weed that it is.

So I have had to develop coping mechanisms to deal with the recurring feeling of doubt and fear. I used education and motivational teachers, as I alluded to before. I gave myself a big-enough why, the "Why do I want to succeed?" question. And once I answered this for myself, it gave me a much bigger reason to pursue my goals rather than accepting the alternative, which is mediocrity for me.

Do you want to know what my why is? It's really simple. It's "Why not?" I couldn't think of a reason that was big enough to not succeed and not chase my goals. Those minor obstacles like not enough money, time, or education or something being too difficult are simply not important or big enough reasons for me to accept being ordinary.

I ask myself why all people cannot come to the same conclusions and can distil the reason down to two factors: self-belief (or lack of) and motivation. And that is the reason for this book.

The Locus of Control

In the1950s, social-psychological learning theory discovered a significant and influential pattern of individual decision making. The locus of control is the degree to which people believe they have control over the outcome of events in their lives, as opposed to external forces beyond their control. This is really significant; therefore, we have to address it because this concept is so powerful that I'll go as far to say that if you don't believe in yourself, you have no chance in self-actualisation and fulfilling those dreams you have for yourself.

What would your world look like if you believed that you were that very vision you have of yourself when you have achieved all of the goals you had ever dreamed of? Are you cruising along the Mediterranean on a superyacht? Are you collecting awards from great institutional bodies for your work? Are you standing atop a podium in first place? What if there were unlimited potential and possibility? What is stopping you? Do you realise that your own self-limiting beliefs are stopping you from getting what you want?

Sequentially this vision comes before your decision point. You have likely thought about what you want in life, but before taking control and making that all-important and potentially life-changing decision, you stop yourself using self-imposed limits. Unfortunately I see this behaviour more often than not.

Let me share something with you. As I have already alluded to, when I was in school, a key person of influence, the headmaster, said not only in earshot but, I am almost convinced, with the absolute intention of me hearing, "That kid isn't going to amount to anything anyway."

I was the only kid in the room while he and another tutor of mine were discussing my behaviour that day. I believed that statement back then as an eleven-year-old. I really did, and it could possibly be that seed of doubt I fight with every day. It was only after joining the British Army that I discovered that success in this world wasn't actually measured in high school exam grades or if you went to university. I discovered that with a bit of self-belief and a little guidance, you could achieve everything you set your mind to.

As I grew in experience in the army but still remained a fairly inexperienced soldier, I surmised that I would do a better job as an officer than I could as a soldier. It suited my personality, and the role complemented my ever-increasing ambition for personal development. So you can imagine my surprise when discussing this with my troop commander, he retorted that I didn't have what it took to be an officer! Talk about high school repeating itself.

I politely disagreed and asked what I needed to do to be eligible to apply for a place in the Royal Military Academy Sandhurst and set out what I needed to do to meet the requirement. I was told that I lacked the education to proceed any further in the application process. That was fair enough. My grades were below average, but I had an irrepressible belief that I was good enough. High school wasn't my time, but now I was ready, and frankly if it were an issue with getting higher grades, that was good news. I could do something about that.

What was potentially a little more difficult was the certain type that the British Army looks for in its officers, a specific level of life experience needed to fit in. Pulling no punches here, Sandhurst is a two hundred-year-old institution that has trained a number of monarchs and political elite across the world. Less than a hundred years ago, it was not only possible but entirely reasonable to buy a commission in the British Army.

So the thought of an uneducated child of the state rubbing shoulders with the middle- to upper-middle class and modern-day royalty is demonstrable evidence that Sandhurst then and today is a learning organisation, forward-thinking, and open to promoting success.

I have nothing but absolute positivity and gratitude for what I learned in the year I spent there from 2005 to 2006 (along with some other well-known students). With that said, I was a bit rough around the edges. I was a product of the state system, with no exposure to cultural pursuits such as going to theatres or art galleries or having social interaction with anyone with an ember of ambition above just getting a job.

But the army had thought of everything. After attending evening school classes for six months, I had boosted my lacklustre high school grades to the minimum level required for entry into Sandhurst. The next steps for me then was attendance on the Potential Officer Development Course, three months of academic, physical, and cultural boot camp.

It wasn't quite *Clockwork Orange*'s famous scene wherein Alex's eyelids are fixed open with some sort of bespoke eye-opening brace, to force him to watch the behaviour-modification films. No, the course wasn't that bad, but it did consist of early starts of around 6:00 a.m. and late finishes at around 11:00 p.m., with weekly trips to the theatre to watch a show, only then to have to write a report on your objective opinion of the show, how you understood it, and if you learned anything from it.

Three months later, I had finished the course and was ready to take my entry exams for Sandhurst. The rest, as they say, is history, but the feeling of completing something that is arduous and difficult is addictively euphoric. Armed with nothing more than self-belief and self-discipline, I was rewarded with what I wanted most at that time, a fair opportunity to apply for a position at Sandhurst.

The short summary of my year's preparation for Sandhurst was challenging in many ways. I did struggle academically. I still do today. I am not the fittest person in the world. I have to work on that all of the time too, but what does come easily to me and what I did have in abundance and remained unshaken throughout this period was belief that I could do it. That was never in doubt.

I have an infinite desire for security, spurred on by the insecurity and poverty of my youth, in environments where ambition and entrepreneurial spirit was the preserve of the other half. Jay-Z, an underappreciated business role model, summarises this beautifully in his track history, where he raps, "All I got is dreams, nobody else can see, nobody else believes, nobody else but me."

My pattern of doubt is not unique; it's the same for millions of people out there. We all have our issues, but what you do about them sets you out from everyone else. Doubt and the influence of the locus of control is my secret weapon. It energises me when I meet irrational resistance to achieving my personal goals. Your beliefs can either hold you back or propel you forward, give yourself time to think about your fundamental beliefs, and ask yourself, "Would the child you once were be happy with the adult you have become today?" Would you encourage a young child to shrink into their environment or burst out onto the world?

Seizing your success, your rightful success, will require you to clarify your vision and surround yourself with people who will support you and believe in you. You are a product of the people you surround yourself with, so take a look at that group. Do you need to change your friend group? Are they taking you closer or further from your dreams? These are challenging questions, and I make no apology. This book hasn't been written to sugar-coat a message. It has been transcribed to give you a simple, honest framework and point of reference for you to use.

I didn't think I was one for daily affirmations. I felt a bit silly saying things like "I am capable; I can succeed" out loud each morning. I don't do any daily chanting, but I do use thought and reflection. Every time I have come up against an obstacle or a challenge that initially may look insurmountable, I reflect on the successes I have achieved so far in life. The army has given me plenty of reference points here, but I am very aware that not every reader of this book will have a military career to look back on.

Don't worry about that. I'm sure there are plenty of examples that with a little help, you could refer back to as significant checkpoints of success in your life. Ask a friend or coworker what they think. You may be surprised. I also use little cues in my life to remind me of my goals. I really love travelling. My wife and I travel as much as we can, and while on the surface of it my goals appear to be rooted in wealth creation for wealth creation's sake, that isn't my goal.

My goal is to facilitate a life of carefree and worry-free travel with my wife, working because we *want* to not because we *have to*. One of my daily cues is the bookmarks I use in the books I read. I typically read two to three books at a time, and in each book, I use a banknote from one of the countries that my wife and I have visited together. I am not a reader of fiction. All of my recreational reading is based on research or personal development. This is both relaxing but purposeful for me. Purposeful relaxing is an oxymoron if I ever heard one.

I will admit that some of the books I read are a little heavy going, and when it does become that little bit harder to turn the pages, I briefly glance at the bookmark and remember where my wife and I were on that holiday, which in turn leads me to think about where we will go next. That brings me back to the book I'm reading and the fact that I'm reading it because it has something to teach me. And so the page turns, and I remain that bit more motivated.

So while I'm not one for daily affirmations, I guess I still use daily prompts to keep myself in check. You may be interested in using them. They are personal to you, so you have to really think about what will light that fire in your belly; however, a good start would be to remind yourself that

1. I can do it; I will do it.
2. I can get better; I will get better.
3. I am committed to achieving/becoming …
4. I can do anything I set my mind to.

Then once you're done and you are reflecting on how far you have come having reached the goals or milestones you set yourself, you get to say:

1. I did do it.
2. I did get better.
3. I became …
4. I set my mind to achieving … and did it.

There is a peculiar side effect of pushing for a goal and then achieving it. What happens is your previously drawn and self-imposed boundaries become a bit bigger because you have become bigger. You have no doubt heard the expression "get outside of your comfort zone." Well, that's exactly what achieving your goals is.

This is, of course, a metaphor as there are no physical boundaries that you must overcome. They are entirely mental ones, and they are the fundamentals of your belief construct. What I would like you to do for yourself is some self-imposed aversion therapy. I want you to select that single thing that makes you doubt your own abilities. Let's say you have a belief that you are not capable of speaking publicly, that the thought of it fills you with fear and you start to feel anxiety. This is a really common fear harboured by millions of people who speak publicly or in front of an audience every day.

I have delivered hundreds of presentations over the years, and I can't think of a single presentation that I have given where I didn't feel nervous. Now I accept that feeling nervous about delivering a presentation is an entirely different proposition in not believing you are able to, so let's address that now with a few easy steps:

1. You can do it, despite what I said about my belief in affirmations above. I do tell myself right before a presentation that I can do this, I'm going to do it well, and these people want to hear what I have to say.

2. Those thoughts you get, the ones where you think you will clam up or people will laugh or question the content of your presentation and make you feel silly, are all thoughts created in the limbic system of your brain called the amygdala. This area controls emotions and triggers that fear. This is a 200,000-year-old part of the brain that was probably useful to early mankind walking the earth. It kept our ancestors alive in precarious situations where the basic fight-or-flight response determined if that person were going to survive. Today, it's less relevant as we have nice, comfortable social structures to keep us all safe, so we need to use our prefrontal cortex for some rational decision-making.

We have been working on this bit of the brain for the entirety of this book so far and will continue to do so. In this part of your brain, your key decisions are made, and planning and personal development synapses are all bursting into life. So if we come back to that dreaded presentation we have to deliver, we can rationally surmise that you can do it, your life is not at risk, and it's more likely that your audience is there to listen to what you have to say.

Not convinced? Remember, you speak in public every day, be that in school, work, at the shops, or socially among friends. So all you're doing is formalising something you do already. What I have done in the past to strengthen my belief that the presentation will be a success is down to preparation and discipline. In the early days of giving presentations, they would typically be quite short, around ten to fifteen minutes.

I would rehearse the presentation several times until I was confident that I would be able to deliver it with only a few bullet points to jog my memory and to make sure I didn't miss a bit of key content. I would then go to the room or space I was delivering the presentation to become familiar with the surroundings and test the IT. I would have a backup plan for how I would deliver the presentation if the IT failed, and I would consider a few questions I would likely get asked at the end of the presentation. Knowing I had done all of this preparation, I believed even more that I could do it. I was confident and felt energised and excited to get started.

This is not only due diligence in the preparation for what you're about to do. It's also the priming of yourself to operate slightly outside of your comfort zone, so when you are exposed for real to the main event, it's not new, it's familiar, and it's something you can deal with and something you can prepare for. Jim Rohn said, "Faith is the ability to see things that don't yet exist, but belief is the knowledge that you can make it happen."

Your skill and your ability is an island of brilliance that you must guard, nurture, and develop. You become what you believe. There is no one else to blame. The decision is yours.

CHAPTER 4

Routine Discipline

Bad habits are easy to form, but hard to live with. Good habits are hard to form, but easy to live with. And as Goethe said, "Everything is hard before it's easy."

—Brian Tracy

I said at the beginning of this book that discipline will be the number-one factor in determining if you will be successful in reaching your goals. We all know what discipline looks like. We all know how easy it is to set a goal and start the process to achieve that goal, but somewhere between the start and the end, something happens or rather stops. Sound familiar? No, how about those New Year's resolutions you set yourself every year? How many have you kept? The emphasis I place on self-discipline cannot be overstated because after all, what else, aside from your environment, do you really have control over?

The word *routine* is an ordinary and uninspiring word because of the context it is normally used. It doesn't inspire a vision of greatness and is probably never used in the same sentence as success, wealth, mastery, or expert. But routine is a very powerful word, and because of routine, people either achieve their successes or not. Routine, as described in the Oxford English Dictionary, means "a sequence of actions regularly followed or performed as part of a regular procedure rather than for a special occasion."

That definition should totally change the way we view the word and how we describe our future actions. I don't consider myself to be exceptionally clever, but I do recognise patterns and try to find causality in the things I see, especially when it relates to human behaviours. With a bit of self-reflection, I recognised early on that my something had to change in my life if I were going to have any chance of achieving my goals. I had set a desired outcome. That was a little more developed from when I was a child. (To be rich, my adolescent vision was not my developed one.)

And while the British Army did a great job in giving me the tools to be a respectable member of society, it stopped short but also never promised in giving me a clear path to wealth. I had reached a decision point and took that decisive decision to leave. My military routines and disciplines were engrained into me as I described earlier, but while these routines and disciplines were and still are sound for achieving success, I was practising them in the wrong environment. So those same routines or disciplines would not take me to where I wanted to be.

So yes, I am saying that the routines and disciplines learned in the military are the same ones I employ today, but what I have changed is the environment I practice them in. The results have been astounding.

Self-discipline has driven mankind to the most incredible of discoveries. You can see in just one example in Thomas Edison's creation of the lightbulb. (Edison found 9,999 ways the lightbulb didn't work before stumbling upon that one prototype that did.[3]) How many times would you have repeated that test? You know by now that the goals you set yourself could range from academic excellence in achieving a degree to adults returning to education or going out for a jog for the first time in years. Your targets could be gaining a promotion at work, losing a few pounds, travelling the world to see exotic lands, seeing spiritual cultures, or becoming the prime minister of Great Britain or the president of the United States. It really doesn't matter. It's whatever you choose it to be.

What matters is your recognition of the absolute need for self-discipline in your approach to reaching your goal. The time has come for me to introduce you to what began as a U.S military efficiency theory, which the Japanese adopted and mastered in the pursuit of industrial and economic excellence. What is this mystery, you ask? Welcome to the kaizen philosophy.

---

[3] It was actually Thomas Edison's team at the Edison Illuminating Company that helped conduct the experiments to find the solution to the creation of the incandescent lightbulb.

Kaizen has various meanings or interpretations depending on which sites your Google search pulls up. For *Decision Point*, I prefer to use the meanings "change for the better" or continuous improvement, as this is the raison-d'être of this book. In my own development, I have used kaizen principles to keep me on the path to achieving all of my goals, short to medium, knowing that the long-term goals will follow. I first read a book written by Dr. Robert Maurer who, in the same way this book focuses on a particular aspect of being successful, encourages the reader to look at the smaller issues that may often go unnoticed and, when addressed, result in dramatic changes.

Everything we have covered so far may still be too much of an effort for some, but not all, but I acknowledge that breaking old routines and habits is incredibly hard. So to give you a helping hand, it's probably best we understand kaizen a bit better.

Now as I alluded to earlier, kaizen was first used for reconstruction of a broken Japanese economy. The Japanese sought "with success" to unite its population and workforce by giving everyone a voice. Think about that. Every member of the organisation has an opinion on how to make things better. For some readers, that may seem quite radical, and for others less so, I guess it depends on the kind and size of the organisation you work for. The magic in this approach leads us to the second part of the kaizen method, to incrementally improve concepts, processes, procedures, and, ultimately, policy.

Anecdotally, there are thousands of workers out there who decry the decisions made by members of their organisation's hierarchy. While one could argue that members of the wider workforce don't usually have access to all of the information available to the board, it stands to reason that the workforce shouldn't really question senior management decisions, right? Well, not always. Do you think that senior management knows the intricacies and processes of all aspects of their businesses? Perhaps not, especially in a multimillion-dollar corporation.

Good ideas escalated to the companies leaders have to go through so many layers of lower to middle management, which is then passed through a bureaucratic sieve, that by the time the idea reaches the board, if at all, it doesn't resemble the original suggestion or intent at all.

So this is where the magic of empowering the workforce multiplies the intellectual capital of an organisation. The best way to see this in action is to look at some real examples. While most will usually associate kaizen with the automotive industry, and Toyota in particular as the first company to use the methodology at scale, I would like to look at other more recent examples. Keep in mind four simple concepts that underpin kaizen success:

1. Involve the whole workforce.
2. Improve processes, systems, or methods.
3. Improvements should be small and incremental.
4. Use teams as the vehicle for change.

Nestlé

This company improved its global production output by focusing on the reduction of waste and better use of space in its factories and resources and talent across its workforce. Internally, Nestlé asked its employees to have a stake in the company and the brand, to be a guardian of the outputs and philosophy, food standard, and compliance. The leadership's top-down approach to improving quality and standards raised the standard across the entire workforce. Promoting a no-waste attitude and constantly looking for ways to improve "as standard" pushed standards higher and increased customer satisfaction.

Standardisation is exactly what routine discipline is. Managers encouraged their teams to seek out minor improvements, and the use of suggestion boxes became a repository for a list of small changes needed to make a big impact. Nestlé also began focusing on internal training and development, a common aspect of modern employment today, but in the 1990s, it was pretty radical. The internal training and development of its own employees is a clear example of the company investing in itself. (Remember, you are your own best investment.) This philosophy proved crucial to Nestlé's continual success as a global leader in food production.

Lockheed Martin

From confectionary manufacturing to defence and aerospace, Lockheed Martin has won notable praise for its results in manufacturing efficiency, but what isn't so widely known is that it used kaizen principles to achieve this. From 1992 to 1997, they were able to significantly reduce errors and defects on their planes down to 3.2. They were able to reduce product delivery time to customers from forty-two months down to less than twenty-two months, and astoundingly they reduced time to move parts and equipment from storage into current stock from thirty days to only four hours.

Lockheed took the view that any member of staff could walk into an area and if they saw something that wasn't right or could be improved upon, they had the freedom to raise this up to their management. It's at this point in most companies where the good ideas stop. Oh, how management becomes the gatekeeper to the successful elevation or rejection of good ideas, but at Lockheed Martin, managers were obligated to report on the outcome of the consideration.

A simple yet powerful requirement was the feedback to the originator of the idea. This 360-degree and whole workforce approach improved processes, systems, and methods at Lockheed Martin. Small and incremental by nature (for a company that employs over 100,000 people globally), Lockheed Martin underpins its team ethos with four key principles in its organisational culture:

1. We, not me: Promoting teamwork
2. Customer first: Thinking about the end state
3. People focus: Thinking about the company's best assets
4. Lead by example: Pride in your work

In both of these examples, the reduction in waste or increase in productivity isn't a huge cost that requires budgeting for. This was a change in mindset and a little consideration and thought about how to improve one small thing. So what does all of this mean for you? What is good enough for large international corporations is good enough for your daily routine.

Nestlé and Lockheed Martin built in routine discipline into their processes. You could call it policy, but policy is little more than a guiding set of principles written down to ensure adherence to a learned or known discipline. This is what you must do to achieve your goals.

So we can see the value in the kaizen method. Let's take a look at how you could apply them to your personal journey. Try these ten small steps to add a bit of kaizen to your life. The beauty of kaizen is if you can't manage to start with all ten, then just start with one and then build on this with another. Your success will be a by-product of the kaizen method and routine discipline.

1.   Wake Up Earlier and Get More Out of Your Day

So this shouldn't come as too much of a surprise, as I used this in an example at the beginning of this book. But whether you're an early riser or not, maximising your day is critically important. I can promise you that no successful individual at the top of their game spends their weekdays getting out of bed late in the morning and taking brunch as their first meal of the day.

Wake up! Inject some energy into your life. Ignite that spark! And if the spark has ignited, then fan the flame. Nobody else can do this for you, and nor should they. You get out of life what you put in, and life will deliver to you what you deserve—good, bad, energetic, or lazy.

2.   Fit in Body, Fit in Mind, Be Healthy

There's nothing attractive in getting out of breath walking up the stairs, and I'm certainly not being judgemental, but first impressions do count. People will simply not take you seriously. If you don't have the self-control to look after your own health, how or why would you expect anyone else to believe you're going to deliver what you say you will?

I am not suggesting you become an athlete (unless that is your principal goal of course), but what I am suggesting is that to be at the top of your game in any field, it will take hard work and mental strength. Your resolve has to be cast iron, and just in case you needed any official medical research, thousands of medical papers and journals positively correlate the body and mind. You are doing it for yourself, and that is selfish, but it's "good selfish," so don't worry.

3.   Be Honest with Yourself

"Could've, should've, would've," these precursors to a sentence stick out like shards of glass when I hear people say them. What I'm thinking when I hear this is, "Well, why didn't you?" I simply do not believe there is a valid reason why that person could not have done what they claimed they could have. This is not being honest with yourself. You can fool others around you, but if you take a moment and ask yourself, "If I really applied myself, could I have done it?" I would bet the answer is yes.

Here are a few benchmarks for you to consider before making any excuses for not following through on a promise to yourself, first some collective benchmarks: Man has walked on the moon, the Egyptians built the pyramids, and the Chinese built a very Great Wall. Individually David Blaine held his breath for over seventeen minutes, Usain Bolt ran 100 metres in 9.58 seconds, and one man, Jadav Paying, planted an entire forest of trees, covering over 1,360 acres by himself. Just imagine the discipline involved in all of these feats. It is astonishing.

As a reader of this book, I suspect you are holding yourself accountable for your actions and taking charge of your future decisions, so just use these examples as inspiration for what you could really achieve if you put your mind to it.

4.   Adapt What Is Useful and Reject What Is Useless

A phrase borrowed from Bruce Lee with a nod to kaizen, this is not about the complete revolution of your life. No, it's about taking the best bits about yourself and enhancing them. There should be a certain amount of correlation to be had with what you are good at and what you most desire to achieve. Goodness knows, if there is, it will be that much easier in achieving those goals. But whether there is or isn't, you should look to your inherent skillset and emphasise those tools to support your journey.

Let's assume that one of your long-term goals is to deliver a TED Talk. (If you're unfamiliar with TED Talks, first I would encourage any reader to indulge, but it is ultimately a presentation to potentially millions of people because they are recorded and live-streamed.)

The one thing holding you back is that you are terrified of public speaking. Ah, OK that could be a problem. But while you are afraid of public speaking, you are very active and vocal on social media forums and groups. So you can communicate and have something to say. Great, let's adapt this, but what is holding you back is self-induced nerves and fear. This is what you reject, and by rejection, I mean you address it and tackle the problem head-on. There are a few ways you could tackle this problem.

First, you could be the first person ever to deliver a TED Talk from behind the curtain of your laptop. Think *Wizard of Oz*. Or probably a little more conventionally, you could take a course in public speaking. Either way, once you have decided to claim your goals, you have to be very active when you come up against hurdles, so use your strengths and aggressively address anything that is of no use to you. Do this and you will feel amazing.

5. Practice, Practice, Practice

Repeated for emphasis, but this is quite self-explanatory. Success is not an accident, and while those who are successful make what they do appear easy, another of the guarantees this book can assert is that it is not easy. Successful people practice, practice, practice. Look at those examples we looked at above, David Blaine, Usain Bolt, or even Jadav. Their successes did not occur when they woke up on a Monday morning. No, in each case, the amount of training, repetition, and discipline is almost beyond comprehension. Practice and discipline are one and the same, kind of like the chicken-and-egg scenario. You can't have one without the other. You must be disciplined enough to keep practicing.

6. Surround Yourself with People Who Represent What You Want to Become

This may not be intuitively obvious to most, as it does require that you step out of your comfort zone. By virtue of you reading this book, I can reasonably presume that you are not surrounding yourself with people who are doing what you aspire to, so start now. When you surround yourself with industry leaders, trailblazers, or those with an insatiable self-belief, it rubs off a bit. It's infectious and forces you to raise your own game. (How fantastic!)

Yes, go to networking events, join a new club, or start an online blog. There are so many ways you can surround yourself with different people nowadays. The internet is a tool to facilitate those all-important connections you need to make. So get out there and build some relationships.

7. Read

There are people out there who since leaving school have not read a book in their lives. This, to me, is self-inflicted intellectual neglect and a sure-fire way to ensure you lack the richness and ability to have a broad and diverse perspective life. There is so much to learn out there. There's too much to learn in one lifetime, but if you focus on those few key things that interest you, this will help you to become a key person of influence, or the go-to person for advice.

I would also recommend reading widely. There is so much insight to be gained from looking at other fields of interest or the way knowledge is gained or applied. To use a very opaque definition, consider the archetypal scientist versus an artist. While both may be industry leaders, their approach to problems would be worlds apart even though they both may arrive at the same solution. You don't have to consume volume after volume of academic text. It's pretty dry at best and at times hard going, but usefully biographies of successful people often provide decades worth of experience and mistakes for you to learn from. If you don't read, you are likely doomed to make similar mistakes unnecessarily.

8.   Remind Yourself of Your Goals Daily and Track Them

Your goals should be an omnipresent kernel in your mind. Hardwired into your psyche, you must remind yourself of what you want to achieve, why you want to achieve it, and how you are going to do it. This will keep you motivated on those difficult days that we all have, where we simply don't feel motivated to get out of bed. Your daily reminder can take the form of whatever you like. Some people speak affirmations out loud; others introspect and take some time to think. A few may daydream. It's a really personal thing and not something I can prescribe what I think will work best.

I prefer quiet time by myself, where I can think about the holistic and all-encompassing plans I have. Writing down these plans is a critical step in achieving your goals because subconsciously you are holding yourself to account; you can use these written plans to refer to daily. Why not stick little reminders on the refrigerator door, be that a list or picture of what you desire the most? I used a notebook for years until I found a software solution that worked for me. Cloud storage is that solution. No matter how many times I upgrade my phone or tablet, all of my information is stored safely in the cloud and I can access it anywhere.

As you remind yourself of your goals, track your progress. Refer back to step number three. Be honest with yourself. Ask yourself, "Did I achieve what I set out to do yesterday, last week, or last month?" If not, why not, and what are you going to do to correct it? This process, this little kaizen step, will keep your discipline levels in the black and ultimately take you that little bit closer to your goals.

9.   Dress for Success

I will use a business example for illustration here, but principally this, along with all of my metaphors and illustrations, can be applied to any skillset. Let's assume that your goal, your desire, is to walk into a boardroom as the chief executive of a big company and to command the respect of your peers through your amazing career and achievements and hold court as you deliver an important piece of good news. But right now, you are just starting out in your new job, with a seemingly impossibly high career ladder to climb before you reach the boardroom. Your colleagues all come to work looking invisibly smart.

There's nothing at all wrong with this, but we are talking about dressing for success here. So you should stand out for all the right reasons. A neat little trick if you don't really know where to begin with buying a new outfit is just to look at the board members. What do they wear? It could be the difference in buying off the peg or treating yourself to something tailored to fit. Or if you really want to make a longer-term investment, then get a totally bespoke suit. Dress with confidence, dress with authority, dress so you feel good, and dress for success. The right people will notice, and before you know it, you will become a person of influence and ultimately on your way to success.

Some industries don't require you to dress formally to climb the corporate ladder. The likes of Google have turned the dress code on its head, so in this case, you should be dressing appropriately for your role. The creatives among you probably don't need a pinstripe either, but like the tech sector, dress for your niche. Treat yourself.

10.   Meditate and Reflect

Sitting cross-legged is not necessary. Just take some time to think. To a certain extent, we covered this in step eight, but this final step is a more developed stage of merely reminding yourself of your goals and the progress you have made to achieving them. Rather than the short-term refection of your achievements and progress, in the same way, we now know that we should set short-, medium-, and long-term goals.

You should also learn how to reflect on your achievements appropriately. Step eight, daily tracking, is more appropriate for short- and, in some circumstances, medium-term goals, depending on how you have defined short and medium term. Meditation and deep reflection are for your long-term achievements and should be holistic and encompass your whole life. We know by now that pursuit of your goals can be interpreted as a selfish pursuit, even if those around us benefit from our success, but periodically taking time to reflect on your whole life allows you to consider wider family, partners, children, friends, and social circles.

Armed with this new considered insight, you get to revisit your decisions to see if they are still the right ones for you. Situations change; therefore so can decisions. John Maynard Keynes is often quoted for saying, "When the facts change, I change my mind."

Misquoted or not, I wouldn't advocate being so wedded to changing my mind just because the situation or facts changed. I would recommend taking that new information and testing that hypothesis. If the decision is still sound, then why change it? Reflection is a really important step along your success journey, so don't overlook it.

Now you have been introduced to a powerful philosophy and seen it applied to both big business and individual target setting. What reason do you have for not moving one step closer to your own goals now? Kaizen is your new secret weapon, and you will know when it's working because somebody will come up to you and say something like, "There's something different about you. Have you lost weight?" This is code for, "You appear to be more confident." Kaizen is your new routine discipline, and with a ten-step framework, what are you waiting for?

CHAPTER 5

Criticism

> Criticism is nothing more than someone's own opinion based on their limitations, listen but don't necessarily believe.
>
> —Nathan John

What is criticism anyway? The definition of criticism for *Decision Point* readers, short and simple, is that it's a "verbal attempt to influence another person." There are other types of criticism of course: food critics, film critics, academic critique, and many more. These, however, are designed to be balanced opinions, but they remain opinions nonetheless.

By now you know and understand how important self-belief, discipline, and leadership is. You also know what habits you need to build into your normal routines to move forward and achieve the goals you have set for yourself. From my own experiences and those who I interviewed for *Decision Point* in chapter 7, I can tell you with certainty that you will face criticism at every stage of your journey. Criticism may not be agreeable, but it is a natural part of your journey toward success, building your character, revealing other people's true nature, and, when proposed constructively, remaining useful in identifying flaws in your plans.

Criticism can be both good and bad. It's oxymoronic in this sense because depending on how it's delivered, who it's delivered by, and how it's received, it may motivate you to push harder and be determined to prove that critic wrong or demotivate you and consign you to a life of certainty and safety that those around you are comfortable with.

What's Wrong with Criticism?

Critical people are victims of their own negativity and have likely had consistent and negative experiences themselves, possibly stemming from childhood, but those negative experiences aren't exclusive to the young. Their own persistent negative experiences will feel like a deep personal inferiority that eats away at self-esteem. This then begins a spiral of self-critique and withdrawal until in full maturity into adulthood. By adulthood, that critique trait is entirely projected outwards to the people they interact with day to day, and you find that a person can become pessimistic, negative, close-minded, and generally unsupportive and even selfish.

Your success journey can be viewed as two sides of a coin; therefore you should be concerned with two factors: your goals and other people's opinions. You have to decide if the argument is balanced and to what extent someone else's opinion will dictate if you will pursue your goals.

We've discussed the importance of goal setting and your personal journey, so now let's look at those irritating and frustrating, but possibly valuable, opinions offered by your critics. Here are some reasons I can think of.

Critics may show you flaws in your work or ambition that you can't see. The purpose of this book is to motivate you into action despite other people's opinions, but sometimes there is value in hearing what others have to say. You must be emotionally mature enough to accept feedback that isn't consistent with what you want to do, but it may just be what you need to hear. Perhaps your critics aren't the best at communicating their concerns or issues they have about your idea or plans, so rather than coming out as constructive criticism or good feedback, their criticism comes out as negative or pessimistic. Read between the lines of what your critics have to say. You understand the wider context and your capability, so pick out the points that are relevant and make a plan to fix the issues.

Your critics might see things from a different perspective, and they bring different experiences when they formulate their opinion. When you're on your success journey, you're likely to be so focused that you become tunnel-visioned and stop making the best decisions that will take you closer to your goal. You should pick up on these risks as you reflect periodically, but just in case you don't, critics may be early road testers of your vision. So if you pause for thought and consider your trajectory from their perspective, you may gain a potentially valuable insight to possible alternative options for your journey. This advice comes with a significant caveat, and that is the context of the situation and who is delivering you that criticism.

In the UK, there is a TV show called *Dragons Den*. (The U.S. equivalent is called *Shark Tank*.) The simple premise of the show is that entrepreneurs across the full spectrum of the business industry enter the "den" and have a few minutes to pitch their idea or business to a panel of wealthy and successful business entrepreneurs. It's a cash investment for a percentage of equity stake in their business. What I enjoy about this show is the panel of successful entrepreneurs are using their own money to invest in the fledgeling entrepreneurs entering the den.

So just like you, if somebody asked you to give them some money, you would likely say, "What is it for?"

The dragons are a little more precise in their line of questioning, and given their years of business experience, they can and do (quite quickly) decide if the fledgeling business is investable from their perspective. They often do criticise a business concept to stress-test the validity of the business model, and for good reason, it's their money. The young entrepreneur has to listen to this criticism, understand it, and either accept it or rebut it.

It's harder than it seems, as some are so wedded to their idea being a success that they aren't able to surrender their own biases and accept the critical points of failure their idea is susceptible to. The result may be a failed business, and years of hard work go down the drain. The converse to this is that while a young entrepreneur entering the den does receive some criticism, they accept the level of risk a dragon investor is taking. So they first accept the criticism as a useful early lesson of issues that need to be fixed before moving forward, and then may offer the dragon investor a larger percentage of equity to compensate for the increased level of risk. The resulting situation is a young business entrepreneur who is financially supported with a wealth of experience to revert to each time there is a decision to make.

Being criticised may be a sign that somebody really cares about you. When you've dared to be different, broken the mould, and pursued your happiness, that can be unsettling for those around you. After all, you are part of their life, their norms, and their comfort zone, so what you do has an impact on them. Caring critics are most likely to be family members, which makes their criticism very difficult to hear.

However, think of it this way. Bill Gates dropped out of Harvard University because he was playing about with a new piece of technology called a computer, of which there was only one in the whole university, because he had a vision of how computers and their software could change the lives of ordinary people. His vision was to put a computer in the homes of every American in the United States.

Can you imagine his parents' horror when he dropped out of one of the world's most prestigious universities to pursue this dream? I don't think that their criticism or displeasure was unfounded. After all, in Bill Gates' case, not only were there no pioneers before him, the technology was restricted to only the top and elite segments in society. I'm sure that the source of their criticism was the love and concern that their young son was gambling his prestigious Harvard degree on. He didn't do too badly.

It's uncomfortable and perhaps even frustrating to have your ideas criticised at all, so when somebody picks holes in your plan for success, it feels like a personal attack. Take a step back and consider two things: how does it make you feel? And what are you going to do about it? The discomfort you feel is when the physical effect of stepping outside of your comfort zone and part of the leadership experience occurs.

Every time you do something new, turn over a new leaf, or do anything to change your status quo, you will feel the same discomfort because your decision is going to impact someone somewhere. Once you have done your research, considered the valid opinions, and listened to your mentor, it's time to make a decision and pursue your goals with conviction! On my own journey, I find that I spend most of my time outside of my comfort zone and expect it to be that way for some time.

When I left the army, I set three-, five-, ten-, and twenty-year goals, all borne out of a decision I took years before leaving. I set these goals to make sure I was both professionally and personally heading in the direction I had mapped out for myself. In the early years of my personal development, I felt slight isolation as nobody else was doing any personal development in the same way I was or certainly for the same reasons. The other unexpected feeling I had was the almost constant self-doubt and questioning if I had made the right decision.

I chose to continue the pursuit of my goals, so I had to address those emotions. The action steps I took was to self-educate because if the doubt were always going to be there, then I had to pacify it with logic, fact, and reason to support my decision so I could continue. This is a similar approach a risk manager takes when trying to mitigate negative occurrences. You do this every day without even thinking about it.

Let's say your goal is to go out and enjoy a nice walk; however, when you look out of the window, you can see the clouds in the sky are grey, and the wind is a bit blustery. You really do want to go out for a walk but don't want to risk getting wet, so you have two options:

1. Go out without your coat and umbrella and risk getting wet (partial success). You did go out for a walk, but you got wet, and now have to dry your clothes. Therefore, you didn't enjoy it.
2. Go out with your coat and umbrella and have peace of mind that you won't get wet (total success). You went out for a walk. It either did or didn't rain, but you stayed dry and warm.

The most surprising thing for me during my last twelve-month service was the criticism to leave and scepticism of my goals. Critics argued that there wasn't anything better as a civilian. I agree military benefits are fantastic. I am a product of most of them. And the sceptics didn't believe the vision I had for myself, and why should they? It was my vision, not theirs. But even so, that's not easy to hear, and as I mentioned in chapter 1, sometimes those closest to you say the things that hurt you most. So for these reasons, your resolve must be solid and unwavering.

Now that we have illuminated some of the benefits of listening to a critic, we should look at some less obvious reasons to ignore critical comments. Here are three I can think of, but I'm sure you will be able to add to this list.

1. If the Criticism Oppresses Your Drive to Move Forward and Makes You Unhappy

If whatever you have planned to do or are currently doing is receiving criticism and you're dealing with it in some of the ways I've covered above, then you should consider that as a step in the right direction. It's normal. The problem arises when you address those areas being criticised, but you're now not happy with the outcome. That's because you are no longer in control of the decision you made and are no longer on the path to success that you envisioned for yourself. You have given over and empowered somebody else.

The art world provides a brilliant platform to analyse a decision maker's decision and the critic's opinion. To simplify the point, let's put ourselves in the shoes of five artists and imagine what their critics might have said about their work.

Leonardo da Vinci

When he painted the Mona Lisa, I can imagine that he received plenty of criticism about his subject. Perhaps she was too pretty or too plain. Maybe the colours weren't correct. The list goes on. But arguably, if da Vinci had listened to his critics, we might not have the Mona Lisa that we enjoy today. What would you have done if you were Leonardo da Vinci?

Damian Hurst

From my own observations, contemporary art divides opinion like no other medium. For some, Damian Hurst is a master of marketing and arguably the publicity stunt. His now world-famous "The Physical Impossibility of Death in the Mind of Someone Living" or "Shark in Formaldehyde" has divided opinion and questioned the very concept and definition of art.

What we don't know for sure is Hurst's original intent. Was it to push the boundaries of what art can be, or was it to provoke a reaction? Either way, he succeeded; therefore those establishment figures who might have criticised the concept privately were proven wrong, and those who have criticised the works since it has been revealed have reduced themselves to nothing more than an irrelevant opinion.

Had Hurst listened to his critics and not produced this piece, how many thousands of people would have not been able to debate his future pieces, and this loss of interest would make the wider art world worse for it. He also wouldn't have the title "world's richest living artist"!

Basquiat and Banksy

Graffiti art has been with us since the homo sapiens drew animals on cave walls. The growth of cities around the world has provided a canvas for the counterculture to express themselves or their ideas in a public space. Despite this, there had never been a crossover into mainstream art. For art snobs, graffiti could never be seen as a credible medium for creating art, and since the late 1970s and early 1980s, that ideology was a self-fulfilling prophecy. Critics usually sitting in socially constructed seats of authority would chastise graffiti art as a nuisance, distasteful, and blemish on an orderly society. In the late 1970s and early 1980s, that all changed when a New York-based graffiti artist named Jean Michel Basquiat exploded onto the scene and into celebrity culture.

Despite this very high-profile graffiti artist infiltrating the upper echelons of the art world, Basquiat's work wasn't mainstream or a household name, partly due to the medium and partly due to the price. In the beginning of his career, he would sell postcards for a few dollars. Now his work reaches values north of $100 million. The other factor was that the art industry was divided on graffiti as a credible medium as a piece of art. That was until the early 1990s when a totally unknown graffiti artist painted a small mural on a wall in Bristol of a girl releasing a heart-shaped balloon. Banksy had arrived.

Interestingly, Banksy has transcended the traditional confines of graffiti art by challenging the establishment, painting politically sensitive and relevant pieces and inviting the public along for the debate. And while they still use spray cans as their instrument, the canvas is no longer exclusively walls and buildings, and we are at a stage where the wider art world is not only accepting of Banksy's work and paying millions of dollars for it, as it did for Basquiat, but you can now find reproduction Banksy works in the homes of millions, tapping into a strong contemporary counterculture.

Had Basquiat or Banksy listened to the critics, the world would be a little less interesting. What of their critics now, I ask you? They are quiet all of a sudden!

Kat Von D

This last artist is slightly different from those above because Kat Von D is a tattoo artist. Tattoos have been a feature in the human race across continents, cultures, and subcultures and can be used to define rank, social status, maturity, personality, and many other descriptors I need not list here. To look at this artist, she is strikingly wedded to her look, with tattoos on most parts of her body, including her face. While Kat Von D hasn't received criticism for being a tattoo artist, she has been criticised for her opinion as a celebrity and the branding of her beauty products created in collaboration with large corporate manufacturers.

Kat Von D was made famous because of her role in a TV show called *LA Ink*. Following her departure from the show, she worked with beauty brand Sephora to create a new line of products that would use her popularity to promote the products. She received criticism at the naming of some of her lipstick products and on several opinions of her social media accounts.

All in all, this artist courts criticism with a pinch of salt, and that's the point of including Kat Von D on this list. Her art isn't necessarily the ink pieces she gives to those who manage to get an appointment with her. For me, it's her irrepressible drive to move forward regardless of her critics. Kat Von D owns her own decisions. You should too.

2.   When Things Get Personal

When you receive the inevitable criticism for taking those steps forward, listen to exactly what is being criticised and who is criticising you. And then consider their motive. Is the criticism about the way you are doing something, your approach to a situation, or is it the size of your vision, belief in your ability, or your well-being?

Broadly speaking, if the criticism ignores your goal, then it's more akin to a personal attack, which should be totally ignored. Why do you think that somebody would aimlessly attack a decision you have made to improve yourself? These people should be given a wide berth, conceptually and in relation to your life-changing decisions and goal setting.

In my experience, when people attack or criticise in this way, it is because of their own personal frustration of not being strong or motivated enough to begin and sustain their own positive change or low self-esteem. In both cases, these people would benefit hugely from reading this book, but I have real concern for those with low self-esteem because it likely stems from a negative experience, and it's the root cause that needs addressing, not just the symptoms. In reading this book and making the decisions you have already started to make, you are becoming a societal change agent, so keep an eye out for those who could use your help. Helping others will help you.

If the criticism you receive focuses on a process or approach of yours and does consider your goals and targets, then this may just be harsh advice. Don't confuse the truth with criticism. We aren't perfect and never will be, despite how good we think we are. The advice you receive from a mentor may seem like criticism, but assuming you have chosen your mentor well, that person has been through what you're going through, and the advice on your processes or approach is likely to be because you could be practicing those things in a more efficient and productive way. Changing your approach or processes may improve your outcomes.

My mentor is very direct. He challenges my logic, and the only critique of my vision is that it isn't big enough or bold enough in his eyes. This is why I spend most of my time outside of my comfort zone, and I do see it as a fortunate opportunity not to be wasted. The key takeaway here is if the criticism threatens to change or alter your decision, such as the size of your vision (being too grand) and your own ability, take a step back and ask yourself, "Who owns my decision? Who benefits from that decision? Am I happy with those answers?"

3. Criticism for Criticism's Sake: Where's the Solution?

Criticism is part of your journey and will be a feature for your entire life. So your mindset should consider it a two-sided coin and therefore should be partnered with a solution. This would then be called constructive criticism and may be worth listening to. If the critique doesn't come with a suggestion for a solution, then that person isn't interested in helping you or is not invested in your project's success. We all know that person at work or college who has nothing positive to say. They may be heard at the water cooler saying, "It will probably get worse … That's a stupid idea … That won't work."

You can probably see that if there isn't a follow-up solution. Then this narrative can be damaging and life-limiting for those with that mindset and those who succumb to that negativity. Let me give you three hypothetical scenarios where we use those three statements above in an unhelpful and debilitating way and again in a constructively critical and helpful way.

Let me introduce you to Alice and Heidi for an example of these two approaches.

Scenario 1: It Will Probably Get Worse

Alice and Heidi are at the watercooler at work and have just come out of a company update meeting with their colleagues in the recruitment department. They have just been told that due to budget cuts, their department has to reduce by 50 per cent or the company, employing several hundred other people, will go into liquidation.

Alice says to Heidi, "I wasn't expecting that. I can't believe it. I have my mortgage to pay. What am I going to do?"

Heidi replies, "I know. Me too. It will probably get worse before it gets better. I bet those in management won't lose their jobs."

This is a real example. How helpful do you think Heidi's response was to Alice? Some things are better left unsaid. Alice more than likely knows that things are going to get worse, but Heidi's comment offers no solution to their problem and adds a speculative and unfounded opinion. As such, the comment has zero value to anybody. What do you think Heidi could have said that would have been better and of more value to Alice? Let's run the scenario again with a more constructive response from Heidi.

Alice says to Heidi, "I wasn't expecting that. I can't believe it. I have my mortgage to pay. What am I going to do?"

Heidi replies, "I know. Me too. It will probably get worse before it gets better, but at least the company is taking action to improve. They are trying to keep the company afloat, and actually they did say that they are increasing the sales department to generate more revenues and increasing the budget for in-house professional development. Shall we sign up for a course?"

I think we can agree that Heidi's response is like night and day here. First, the tone is positive, upbeat, and future-focused. Heidi offers some extra information about increasing the sales department and the offer of professional development for all staff. This immediately gives Alice some positive options to think about to help solve a potential problem and will therefore change their mindset to being solution-focused rather than a depressive.

Some people in the world are fundamentally optimistic; others are more pessimistic. You have to find it in yourself to be the former, and now that you know the impact of the alternative, what's the point in being a pessimist? Really? To be a pessimist is closed, limiting, and restrictive; being an optimist, even if wrong or in the face of adversity, is open, progressive, and positive. What would your immediate response have been?

Scenario 2: That's a Stupid Idea

Let me tell you about some other stupid ideas that were heavily criticised.

Talkies

"What are talkies?" I hear you say. Well, you probably know it better as a theatre or cinema. Hollywood movies are a part of modern life, with movie franchises for everybody covering romance, action, horror, and sci-fi. But in the early 1900s, movies were nothing more than a series of flickering pictures with no sound. It wasn't until 1927 and the release of a movie called *The Jazz Singer* starring Al Jolson that the world would have a cinema experience akin to what we all know and enjoy today. As with any advancement in technology or change to the status quo, *The Jazz Singer* received its fair share of critique, but not for its content. It was the medium of moving pictures itself.

The president of United Artists went on record in an interview with *The New York Times* saying that synchronised audio was just a gimmick and wouldn't last.

Television

Ubiquitous across the world, television is a focal point in the homes of billions of people around the world, but even the TV was a stupid idea at one point. In the late 1920s and early 1930s, television was in its infancy, and as with all pioneers, the idea was ridiculed. Experimental broadcasts began in the mid-1930s when most households had a wireless (radio), so in a 1939 editorial in *The New York Times*, it stated that the TV would never be a serious competitor for radio because people must sit and keep their eyes glued on a screen. The average American family hasn't the time for it. With this damning indictment, the TV was consigned to history. Of course it wasn't. It's another example where critics have gotten it completely wrong.

The Internet

The internet has actually been with us for decades longer than we realise, albeit in a non-commercial form. Arpanet was the first working prototype for communicating over a network, allowing more than one computer to talk to another. Fast-forward to the 1980s and the early commercialisation of the technology because the concepts were so esoteric and you literally had to speak another newly invented language. Computers were too niche for the majority in society.

By the mid-1990s, the technology had started to penetrate the homes of the middle classes, and it wasn't uncommon to see dial-up computers in people's homes, but that didn't stop commentators from criticising the viability of the internet. Books were published that predicted the failure of networked computing, with one particular author stating that e-commerce would never succeed.

The point here is that an idea is only stupid to those without the vision required to see it through to its full potential. If that idea is linked to your dreams, most will not share your vision, so you must have complete belief in yourself. There are countless examples in popular culture of celebrities from various industries who were ridiculed for pursuing their passion, who then went on to be a captain of their industry.

Scenario 3: That Won't Work

There's a rich history of early electricity pioneers. The credit of discovering the nature of electricity is attributed to Benjamin Franklin following his famous kite experiment. But in reality, knowledge and experience of the existence of electricity can be dated back as far as 2750 BC in Ancient Egypt. Fish they called "thunder in the Nile" were described as protectors of the fish and prevented overfishing.

Fast-forward to the early nineteenth-century, modern heavyweights including Alexander Graham Bell, Thomas Edison, Galileo Ferraris, and Nikola Tesla had turned electricity from a peculiar scientific curiosity into an everyday essential utility of modern life. Tesla is the subject of this example.

He was born July 10, 1856, in what is modern-day Croatia and pioneered alternating current (AC). Most of his futuristic ideas came from visions rather than conventionally written notes and thoughts. Never rushing into actual work, he assembled his ideas piece by piece in his imagination first, where he would change the construction and improve his devices all in the metaphysical and at no cost, less for an extraordinary mental agility required for such complex computation.

Working for Edison Corporation, he moved to the United States and ended up working with Thomas Edison himself. While the two electro pioneers shared mutual admiration for scientific progress, tension began to present in each individual's approach to the best method of transmitting electricity, alternating current (AC)(Tesla) or direct current (DC) (Edison).

Edison was all too aware of the commercial benefit of harnessing the power of electricity, and as such, he had taken out patents for the transmission and use of DC power as a viable mass-produced commodity. Knowing that AC was a real threat, Edison sought to discredit Tesla and his inventions, and with strong commercial support from investors and buy-in from the closed American scientific community, Edison won.

It is not an exaggeration to say that Nikola Tesla is the father of modern-day radio (not Marconi), mobile phones, wireless transmission, and hydro-electric generators. The pursuit of science, not wealth, was Tesla's goal. Wealth was the material target of Edison and his company, General Electric. Tesla's commercial savvy, not his ideas, was his downfall. We use AC in our homes today. I am delighted that we are still reaping the altruistic and egalitarian benefits of Nikola Telsa today, channelled through the equally misunderstood Elon Musk.

Musk has literally turned the internal combustion engine automotive world upside down with the creation of a car, the namesake of our champion. The Tesla is the twenty-first century's Ford Model T and soon-to-be disruptor to global energy supply and eventually the migration of mankind onto other planets.

How to Deal with Criticism

I'd suggest accepting that criticism is a normal part of your personal development journey. By accepting this, you'll understand that you don't always have to have an answer for your critics. You don't have to feel guilty for wanting to do something for yourself, and you shouldn't think that what you're doing is wrong.

So here are some practical tools you can use for dealing with criticism. You don't have to use them all.

1. Check the critic's credibility. Are they credible, and what is their opinion worth to you?
2. Determine the critic's intent? Are they concerned for your best interests, or are they measuring your dreams based on their own limitations?
3. Breathe. It's not nice to be criticised. Don't overreact. Taking time to compose your thoughts before your actions will empower you immeasurably.

4. Listen. If the criticism is based on a falsehood, ignore it. If the criticism is based on truth, analyse it, understand the facts, and adjust your plans.
5. If the criticism is an attempt to prevent you from moving forward toward your life goals, ignore it.
6. If the criticism erodes your sense of self-worth, ignore it.
7. Learn from it. It's not the last time you're going to be criticised.
8. Use it to solve problems.
9. Recognise that you will find criticism outside of your and other people's comfort zone.
10. Use it to identify weaknesses in your ideas and plans.
11. Recognise that praise is good and constructive criticism is excellent. Grow from it.
12. Act. Don't dwell on it. The more time you spend worrying, the less time you spend developing and improving.
13. Separate your emotions from the criticism. You'll make better decisions.
14. Recognise that social media is a double-edged sword. It's excellent for feedback, but make sure you benchmark opinions and criticism against point one.
15. Ask if yourself if you secretly agree with the criticism. Someone says to you, "You're really disorganised. How are you going to …" if you agree, this is shining a light on an issue that you really must address. Criticism isn't always bad.

Nobody's perfect. Just do your best.

CHAPTER 6

Students, Teachers, and Everyone Else

When the student is ready, the teacher will appear.

—The Buddha

I consider success to be a by-product for those who recognise that they always have something to learn. I don't mean that you should spend the rest of your days learning everything there is to learn in the whole world; therefore it will follow that you will be successful. No, that would more likely result in an intangible accumulation of a broad, general knowledge that could only be applied on TV game shows.

What I am suggesting is all of the most successful people in the world share one common feature, a continued desire to learn. Learning is deep and expands into areas with an effect on that individual's area of expertise.

Take Bill Gates, for example, founder of Microsoft and now philanthropist. He is a voracious reader. He has himself confessed to setting aside at least an hour each day for reading, and while in his early days founding, establishing, and growing Microsoft, that reading might have been quite technical and IT-specific. As a philanthropist, Bill and his wife, Melinda, have turned their attention and therefore recreational reading and research to a broader area of application. They have now turned their attention growing the Bill and Melinda Gates Foundation.

The motto of the foundation is intentionally vague, "All lives have equal value, we are impatient optimists working to reduce inequality," but the allocation of the foundation's massive cash reserves (north of $50 million) is tightly linked to the legacy knowledge, deep research, and understanding of Bill Gates' altruistic interests.

Warren Buffett, co-owner of the most valuable investment company in the world, Berkshire Hathaway, is famed for spending almost all of his entire day reading, hoping to learn a little more! This is despite being in his eighties and a highly successful billionaire. He still believes he has much to learn. Imagine that. Interestingly Bill Gates considers Warren Buffett his mentor, and they both enjoy almost daily calls to discuss globally significant issues and how to solve some of the world's most challenging humanitarian crises.

Together, these behemoths of the global have formed "The Giving Pledge," a campaign that seeks to encourage the already wealthy to contribute the majority of their wealth to philanthropic causes. The pledge has over two hundred signatories from individuals, couples, or existing foundations, and so far it has over $500 billion worth of pending donations.

The Giving Pledge doesn't actually spend any money; nor does it dictate how it should be spent, but it's a great first step in solving some of humanities' most challenging problems. Warren Buffett has already pledged 80 per cent of his net worth to the Bill and Melinda Gates Foundation, whom he sees as a better custodian for the distribution of this massive wealth.

A slight journey off-topic, but for such a worthy and noble cause, I think it was worth it. The point I was trying to make when citing Bill Gates and Warren Buffett is that society would judge these two men as having made it. What could they possibly have to learn? But I use their example to show you (and I practice what I preach here) that you are and will always be a student, which is a very good thing. Gates and Buffett are two of the most successful businessmen in the world, and they consider themselves as students!

So are you convinced that you have more to learn? You are a student. You are a student in life, you are a student in your profession, and you are a student learning and planning to achieve your goals. Continual professional and personal development will help you to stay current and relevant in your field. I can think of countless analogies, as I'm sure you can too of people and companies that fall from the lofty heights of success, once occupying a position of success and prosperity to one of depression and failure. This lack of progression besets huge companies as well as individuals.

Consider the dominant market position occupied by the likes of Blockbuster VCR rentals. They never thought that DVDs would take off, but think about what companies like Netflix or Amazon have done to the movie and TV rental market.

The reality is that Blockbuster should have been much more forward-leaning and progressive enough to make an entry into the rental market extremely difficult by leveraging its market share. It didn't, so it fell. The same happened to Blackberry. For those old enough to remember, this company was *the* phone to have. It was a mini-computer and barometer for success for professionals. For the wider, more lucrative consumer market, Nokia was a behemoth churning out handsets and market-leading in making cell phone access more affordable to the mass market. The iPhone crushed both.

Ask yourself how it could have been possible for a computer manufacturer to enter a market it had no experience in at all and was able to topple the two largest firms in the telecoms industry. The answer is a simple one: Blackberry and Nokia did not continually develop. They rested on their laurels and allowed Apple, a visionary company, to push the envelope of what was possible to a point where Blackberry and Nokia could no longer compete.

As I mentioned previously, this same development philosophy is an unwritten rule for individuals too; however, not wanting to be critical or derogatory of a person, I would much prefer to champion the success of those people who have continued to develop themselves and stay relevant.

How many celebrities can you think of who have stayed relevant or in the public eye for more than ten years? I have to say that I am quite impressed by a few in the entertainment industry. Of note, Madonna, Kylie Minogue, Tom Jones, and the Rolling Stones have evolved over the years to meet the changing needs of a new fan base while retaining the loyalty of their early supporters. They have almost become part of the furniture in the music landscape and have been present in our lives for over thirty years, and this has been achieved by an understanding that their audience has changed.

They were students, and their fans were the teachers. They changed stylistically by creating new trends for others to follow (a particular position of strength) and musically where they have either kept pace or decided to master a genre. Can you think or a more accomplished rock band than the Rolling Stones? While I accept they have developed less in style, their position at the zenith of the rock music hierarchy is (and I doubt will ever be) under threat.

In the 1980s when New Romantic pop was all the rage, all of these artists were present and relevant. Madonna, in particular, saw success with her semi-erotic videos, but she recognised a change in audience trends and the influence of drum and bass becoming more present in popular culture. As a result, Madonna released a successful drum and bass single. She didn't stop there. You may even remember her departure from drum and bass into pop, and then out of nowhere she released to high acclaim "Don't Tell Me," a country and western single! Like her or not, Madonna is a master of reinvention.

Other singers who can claim similar success include Kylie Minogue with corny but very commercial pop culture music, but a move into dance music was a step-change in her traditional audience. She learned and evolved. And Tom Jones's résumé speaks for itself. He's been in the business for over fifty years and is still present on TV today as an icon and industry leader. These artists were all masters of their instruments but students to the industry.

Sports is a particularly impressive area because of the physical demands placed on sportsmen and women as they compete at the highest levels. Their bodies absorb a significant amount of stress, and they are also susceptible to the normal body's ageing process. This is why I find consistent sporting success over decades a significant achievement. Consider these examples. In tennis, Serena Williams has dominated the game for fifteen years, competing well into her mid-thirties. And after becoming a mother, Serena continues to be the benchmark for conversation and competition in the women's game. She has maintained this level by being disciplined enough to continually learn about the game and changing the way she trains and lives as her natural biology changes. It's not an easy thing to do at all.

Roger Federer is the same. He not only continues to win Grand Slam titles (twenty championships at the time of writing), and in each of these competitions, he dispatches with younger and arguably fitter competition. His desire to learn has kept him in the top tier of the men's game.

I have shed some light with a few examples of how important it is to continually develop yourself. You get to choose if you want to be a student and the prize at the end. Well, it's not a piece of paper that reduces in value over time. (Just how valuable are your high school grades when you are forty-five years old?)

Your prize is the development of yourself, your business, and a perpetual value that you can translate and relate to any situation you happen to be in for the rest of your life. That could look like a skill that you develop, improving areas of your work, predicting how a situation may pan out based on your own experiences, or just being able to hold a broader conversation because you have a wider knowledge to draw on. You win every time!

Teachers

One of the reasons for writing this book is because of the lessons I was taught both formally in school and socially by my surroundings as I grew up. How things have changed over the decades! My oldest memory of teachers is of an old man or woman at the front of the classroom, standing in front of the blackboard, chalk in one hand and board rubber in the other, going on and on about a subject I had no interest in and couldn't see the relevance of that subject in my life at that moment.

I remember science teachers coming into lessons, turning to the blackboard, and then proceeding to write on it for one hour and instructing us to copy the text, go home, and revise it! Seriously! Seriously? How is that supposed to be inspiring?

Reflecting on this now, I ask myself, "To what extent was it my fault that I didn't learn anything?" I wasn't a bad kid. I was just not interested, but I refer you back to chapter 2, where we discussed that the drivers and responsibility for child-to-teenage learning lie with the institution, not the individual. After all, the institution is there to teach.

My main issue with Western teaching philosophy is that it teaches the wrong thing and is too results-driven. I do understand that there is an economic need to have a reasonably educated workforce to continue to drive the economy, but I think that teaching a specific subject matter is less important than the option to teach someone the love of learning or how to learn. If you love learning or know how to learn, the subject matter is more easily absorbed. Thus you become a better product as a result. In my case during my adolescence, the student was ready, but the teacher did not appear.

I do think you can be both a teacher and a student, and you too should aspire to be both. Each step you take, be that forwards or backwards, is a movement that someone else can learn from, yourself included.

So let me try to redefine what I think a teacher should look like. First, they are there to inspire, which is a deeply personal thing. How many people inspire you? And what is it about those people who draw you in? I find inspiration in the very primal traits of courage and persistence. Some would call it the struggle, but that isn't true. The struggle is the vehicle we can all relate to and is not limited to trying to get good grades at school or find a job, getting promoted in your work, paying off your mortgage, managing difficult relationships, or dealing with bereavement.

This is life, not a struggle. What I admire are those who attack life with energy and are relentless in the pursuit of living and the absolute rejection of being a passenger or a victim. That energy fuels my disciplines, which my kaizen practices reinforce, which are now driving me to share my experiences and thoughts with you.

Second, teachers are there to pass on knowledge. I mean, if you're not passing on knowledge, then by definition, you can't be a teacher. Even if the thought of teaching or mentoring doesn't come naturally, remember that I am trying to break down those preformed conceptions of what you may think a teacher or mentor looks like. I'll let you into a secret: there are no teacher templates. You already are one!

Don't believe me? Just pause for thought for a minute. How many times have you burned the midnight oil in an effort to get an assignment for a deadline? Have you ever purchased something purely on impulse and regretted it? Have you ever made a bad decision?

I could go on, but what I'm getting at here is that these are lessons that you have already learned and that someone else out there can benefit from your experience if you share it. It might be a family member or a coworker.

It really doesn't matter. Remember, there might just be someone out there whom you inspire.

Finally I think that teachers and mentors are there to support the student. This is a longer-term relationship rather than just the immediate passing on of knowledge or information. As we age, we tend to refer to teachers as coaches and mentors. Both are different in what they aim to achieve, but both teach a student in one way or another.

I'll define each so you'll be able to recognise what these people are there to do for you because some would argue that they occupy the same development space. Coaches and coaching is a multimillion-dollar industry because corporate and professional-level businesses and industries recognise the value to be gained by taking somebody's prior experience and using it to help someone less experienced on a task or their performance. It's like short-term medicine for a problem and is usually more professionally focused.

Mentoring, on the other hand, aims to build a capability and draw out an individual's inherent strengths. What isn't commonly known about mentoring is that the mentor is likely to be gaining from the relationship too! Mentors are the epitome of the "student of life" philosophy. This is why Bill Gates and Warren Buffett continue to build their relationship well beyond that of any financial metric. They both benefit from the sharing of wisdom, and this is why they continue to read broadly and widely.

Both coaches and mentors will share a certain set of qualities, some of which I have listed subsequently. I say some because it's not a checklist but will give you a sense of what would make a good coach or mentor:

- Committed to personal development and help others do the same
- Good listeners
- Empathetic and understanding
- Good at building relationships
- Builds a student's confidence
- Challenges the individual
- Encourages reflection
- Helps the student to think differently
- Share experiences
- Relationship-focused, not goal-focused

With these three qualities in mind, let me share with you two examples of my own experiences in understanding this dynamic, the first being a typical student-teacher relationship and the second a little bit more unusual.

I have a military history, and the organisational structures are very hierarchical. So more often than not, sadly, intelligence and ability are incorrectly correlated to the ranks that an individual hold. You know the drill. When I say "jump," you ask, "How high?" Before I go on, it's worth framing the context of this example by explaining the rank structure in the British Army.

Soldier Ranks

- Private Soldier: First rank, all new soldiers start here
- Lance Corporal: Junior team leader, first non-commissioned officer (NCO) rank
- Corporal: Team leader
- Sergeant: Senior team leader
- Staff/Colour Sergeant: Junior manager
- Warrant Officer (Class 2): Middle management (holds a royal warrant)
- Warrant Officer (Class 1): Middle management (holds a royal warrant)

Officer Ranks: All Commissioned by the Monarch of the Day

- Second Lieutenant/Lieutenant: First rank, all new officers start here (Royal Military Academy Sandhurst graduates, think of this as a leadership fast track or executive stream)
- Captain: Junior manager
- Major: Middle/upper middle management
- Lieutenant Colonel: Senior management
- Colonel: First of the army staff ranks, the organisational administrative executives in the British Army; these are policy and doctrine roles.

- Brigadier: Senior management
- Major General: Executive
- Lieutenant General: Executive
- General: Executive

So following this whistle-stop tour of ranks in the British Army, I will proceed with my short story. Having left school at sixteen with little to no GCSEs to speak of, joining the army was an excellent way for me to learn a little discipline and do some personal development, all while I decided what I wanted to do with my life.

Example 1

After basic training as a private soldier, I persevered in my job, doing as I was told, as all good soldiers should do, and taking orders from my superiors. But there was a problem. More often than not, I found myself questioning, internally of course, the logic and sense of some of the tasks we were being asked to do. I also found that as time went by, I began to listen more intently to how I was being asked to do things, and in the military, as some readers will know, you aren't often asked to do things. Rather you are told in no uncertain terms with no opportunity to offer an alternative suggestion.

There is good reason for this absolute obedience. Having served multiple times on overseas operations from 1999 to 2011 in conflict zones, there really isn't time to be debating if something is a good idea or not. Lives are literally at stake, so team safety and the mission are the priority. That is why military leadership can be so opaque. This leadership is built on training, repetition, and experience, so it follows that the more time you spend in the military, the more training you undergo, the better at being a professional soldier or officer you will become.

Soon after completing my basic training, I began almost immediately applying for personal development courses. I couldn't believe the opportunities in front of me. I had an employer that encouraged learning and development and was willing to pay for it. Having come from a situation where there was no opportunity, I couldn't get enough. Anything would do—IT courses, health and safety courses, and presentational techniques courses. You name it, I'd do it.

You could be forgiven for thinking that my time for learning and development had come, but I don't think it was so much that the time had come. I think it was the way training, learning, and development was executed in the military. It suited me better. Although at the time I didn't realise it, I had accepted that I was a student, I was ready to learn, and I understood that I was surrounded by potential teachers: people who inspired me to want to become a better soldier and a better person, people who were obligated by their position to teach me how to be a better soldier, and people who wanted to support my development as not only a soldier but my personal development as well.

This was the catalyst that lit my desire to learn. I discovered how to learn, and now I couldn't get enough. I wanted to know more about everything because I got a thrill from knowing something new that I didn't know the day before. This desire has continued to this day, but it's just a bit more focused now and purposed to help me to achieve my own life goals.

During my army years, I wasn't really conscious of the self-management skills I had developed. Learning had just become part of my routine, almost second nature. As I improved my business (me), I wasn't only keeping pace with my peers at work, but I was operating at a higher level and higher outputs. I was thinking differently, and most importantly my new insights were pushing my ambitions further and further every day. I had been promoted twice (to corporal) ahead of my peers, but the fixed criteria and eligibility time frames were pedestrians in comparison to the pace I wanted to develop.

I began to get frustrated; I still get frustrated today if I'm not developing, much to the frustration of those around me. But for me, reading, learning, and development are relaxing. This is where the internal conflict began for me. Notwithstanding the operational imperatives of leadership, my issues were all about peacetime and in barracks inefficiency. And without turning this book into a bio, I had decided that the time had come for me to leave the army!

Yep, I had lost respect for my middle management and even for my troop commander, and I now believed that I could do a better job and wasn't prepared to wait the fifteen years it would take in the military framework to reach the ranks I'd need to, to be able to affect positive change.

A chance meeting with a captain who had just arrived at my unit changed all of that. He had once been a soldier himself and explained to me that with some rigorous testing, there was a way for me to leapfrog all of the soldier ranks and have the opportunity to try for a place as an officer cadet in the Royal Military Academy Sandhurst training, but it wouldn't be easy. He, AKA Captain Charlie, was a seasoned, experienced officer who was in charge of the vehicles and maintenance of the vehicle fleet in my regiment, which was no mean feat. This numbered around four hundred vehicles. (Back then, these vehicles were not quite a modern vintage, but vintage is the right word to use!)

Not only would I have to pass the quantifiable academic and physical tests, but I would have to overcome the biases and culture in the army at that time. In my opinion back then, the officer class was thought of as being more refined than the soldier ranks. Think *Downton Abbey.* You don't see soldiers sitting down to dinner among the landed gentry. This was for an officer. This was for ladies and gentlemen.

My hard-fought qualifications earned in Wednesfield High School were hardly enough to get me through the gates of an institution with the history and prestige of Sandhurst. I had to really scrape the intellectual barrel here and convince my superiors that those old-school certificates had no bearing on my desire and attitude anymore. This took some convincing, and I do understand why. The typical candidates for Sandhurst were university graduates who had broader life experiences than I had at age twenty-two. There was a risk that I would be overwhelmed by the mental stresses put upon all cadets during the nine-month commissioning course.

So yes, my paper qualifications were in the red. I was overdrawn in my academic account, and I had a massive deficit to make up. But what I did have was a relentless ambition to succeed and knew that if I got into Sandhurst, then I would complete the commissioning course and pass out nine months later as a commissioned officer.

With the support of a teacher and now mentor, Captain Charlie, I submitted my application for a commission, which surprised everyone in my troop. I am eternally grateful to Captain Charlie because of the time and mentorship he gave me at a time when I needed it most. Captain

Charlie listened to me, he was empathetic and understanding as he had been a soldier himself before, and he helped me build my confidence and self-belief by setting me tasks and duties over and above what I or any of my peer ranks would be expected to do, like organising large events and public speaking. He constantly challenged me and asked what I thought I could have or would have done better if I had the opportunity to do a task again.

It's worth stating that reflection is one of my most valued personal strengths to this day. Reflection is very different to reminiscing. It's not looking back through rose-tinted specs; nor is it a subconscious arbitrary activity. Reflection is an active pursuit, a critical analysis of a task or experience you have done or had with a view to learning from your mistakes, identifying what did and did go well, and improving on your decision-making ability in the future.

Captain Charlie showed me how to think differently. He showed me how officers think, taking a step back and elevating your thinking and horizon scanning to formulate strategy. All of the time he did this, he shared his own experiences from his journey from soldier to officer. I made the decision to become an officer. I made no secret of it, and my teacher appeared. And after the physical, mental, and academic on the Potential Officer Development Course, I made it to Sandhurst in September 2005 and subsequently passed out as a Second Lieutenant in August 2006.

For a soldier to take these steps is a rare event. In my intake at Sandhurst in September 2005, there were 220 cadets, and only 10 of us were ex-soldiers trying to commission from the ranks (4.5 per cent). To add a bit more context to those figures, at the time, the army was circa 80,000 strong in 2005, and of all of the soldiers who made it to the Potential Officer Development Course, I was one of twelve. That's less than 1 per cent (0.015) of the whole army. It's beholden of me to state that not everyone had applied to become an officer and there are plenty of other courses that I would not be cut out for, but you get the point.

It would have been very easy for me to rest on my laurels at this point. After all, I had advanced my career by fifteen years in less than a year. I had made it to the executive stream where opportunities would be more varied and interesting and my progression would only accelerate from here. I was on the executive stream for higher management, and in my mind, the world was my oyster. I didn't rest on my laurels, as my curse struck again.

While at Sandhurst, I felt intellectually inadequate among my peers. Degrees at that time were still relatively rare, and it was not the norm for people from my social background to attend university. I thought that graduates were super smart, the types that aced all of their exams in primary school. Higher education for me was reserved for those in higher society. I found myself thinking that if I could make it to Sandhurst and pass the course with all of these super-smart graduates, then a degree couldn't be that difficult surely.

So I leapt in with both feet and enrolled in my first-degree course in politics, philosophy, and economics. I had developed my ability to learn, and all this did was feed my irrepressible desire to want to learn, the perfect combination for me, because I loved learning new things.

This ends my first example of the benefits of a good teacher. Had I not met Captain Charlie, I wouldn't have had the confidence or vision to take the career decision I did. Whether or not he recognised himself as a teacher is irrelevant (and he probably didn't), his actions made him an excellent teacher and mentor to me. He inspired me with tales of his own journey. He passed on his knowledge of his journey and what he knew of the process of becoming a commissioned officer.

And finally he supported me during my year of pretesting to become a candidate for Sandhurst. I am eternally grateful for this, as he was an architect in the changing of my life. I only hope I can emulate his example with my actions in life and help somebody else on their journey. Becoming an officer was my goal and target from 2001 to 2006, and I achieved it.

What is your goal? What have you written down? With the passage of time, some willpower, and determination, you will reach your success too.

Example 2

You're now better able to put into context my mindset back then, having seen how my background has been shaped. I was at a point where I felt I could accomplish anything. I was in the army and pumped full of confidence, possibly borderline arrogance, and now I sought out a long-standing desire. I would now plan to move into a new chapter in my life and lifestyle. This was going to be my wealth creation phase.

I had little knowledge of wealth or even how to define it, let alone an understanding of what an asset or liability was. This is kind of entry-level stuff if you want to become wealthy, as I did. However, this retrospectively understood lack of knowledge wasn't as clear to me back then as it is now. So the limited surface-level information I did know about investing I thought would stand me in good stead. In reality, it was little more than a generalist consumer-level knowledge, and the only thing that separated me from the general population was that I was actively involved in my own personal finances, but by no means a specialist.

I liked the idea of day trading on the stock market to supplement my income. Some readers of this book are probably nodding right now. After all, we've all seen the movies. "Buy low, sell high," I hear you say. I saw a way to easily generate more money each day than I earned as a salary and eventually becoming financially free. My vision (modest of course since I'm not a megalomaniac) was of living in a detached house surrounded by fields. Next to which would be a small clutch of outbuildings, one housing my office where I did all of my serious day trading, which would be anchored by a desk and a multi-screen computer and a couple TVs with different news channels on, so I would be to-the-second updated on world events that I could capitalize on to boost my profits for the day.

I can almost see your face now. I'm pulling the same one, so cliché. The second of those outbuildings would be my car garage, where I would retire to after an hour's trading to select a car that took my fancy so I could go on a nice afternoon drive. Naturally when I got bored with all of that, three or four times per year (or at the drop of a hat), I would find myself on holiday in far-flung places around the world with my better half.

Not a bad vision, I'm sure you'll agree, but this was the level of detail that was painted in my vision. It wasn't a want. It was a need. And when things got tough in the following months and years, this vision would eradicate procrastination and fire up my motivation reserves.

It's a small segue into my mindset, but it does show you what my motivation really was when I refer to it as wealth creation. There was a problem. I was totally ignorant to just how broad a subject and indeed how much work investing could be. Thousands of finance professionals around the world lose money every day in carrying out investment activity in their specialist areas they are trained in, so how on earth could I possibly think that I would be able to dabble and make a success of it? Confidence, misplaced, yes, but confident nonetheless.

So buoyant with confidence, I read a few books and took the plunge. I lost money quickly! Traders and investors among you, I can hear you laughing. I have to say that I chuckle myself now too. In retrospect, despite my experiences, I didn't recognise that I continued to repeat mistakes, and I didn't do any research or analysis. It was all gut feeling, and any trader or investor will tell you. Even if you get a bit lucky (and it will be luck) the first time or even the first few times, you will not succeed in the finance game with gut feelings.

What I needed was a teacher, a mentor, someone to show me the ropes, to show me how to focus my efforts for better results. I wasn't work-shy, and I was willing to put in the hours of personal development. After all, by this time in 2012 I had completed three degrees. So while I was actively looking for the right teacher/mentor, I was searching in the wrong places. I was seeking amongst peers and, worst of all, internet trading and investing bulletin boards. Yuk.

Around midway through 2012, I was in a captain, a middle management position in the officer executive stream. I had a staff of twenty-two people, and professionally I could want for nothing more, but personally I still felt a little unfulfilled. I was about a year into my investing career and had learned a few key fundamentals, so all things being equal, I'd say I was about flat. The gains covered any losses I had made over the year. At the very least I wasn't losing money.

I had also developed a bit of a reputation for being the bloke who wanted to be a millionaire, and word spread. You put it out there, and the universe will respond. One of my employees, a corporal, had heard that I was investing in the stock market and approached me to see what kind of investments I had.

This took me by surprise, as I was in no way expecting a junior work colleague to have an interest in investing. (It wasn't something that had ever been discussed in my whole career.) Nor did I expect that intellectually he would be as visionary as what I had become. Even amongst my peers, I felt a little more strategically focused because I had planned my life well beyond the army and was not taking internal promotion too seriously anymore. This soldier of mine had taken an interest because he himself was a much more accomplished investor than I was and had been investing and trading on the stock market for years.

I will say that if you trade on the stock market for years as an amateur, you are doing pretty well, as it's a very unforgiving arena as most lose most, if not all, of their money within six months. So this guy had a stable, sustained, and disciplined method to stay in the game and make it worth his while.

When the student is ready, the teacher will appear. I was ready. Corporal Grand (not his real name) blew me away with his understanding of investing and immediately gave me a reading list of books that I had to read if I were to have any chance of becoming successful in investing in the stock market. I was ecstatic. You don't know what you don't know, but when you do know what you don't know, that was a very exciting place to be for me.

I devoured each book, and as I did, my mind became more tuned to my preferred style of investing, considering my aims, time scale, type of investment, and risk. I had found my path to the wealth I had dreamt about for years.

I cannot overstate how unlikely it is that in a military environment, an officer would take tutorage from a soldier. I am aware how this may sound to anyone who hasn't served in the military, but the do-as-I-say culture is necessarily linked to rank, as I covered previously.

Perhaps it was my own background as soldier that opened my mind to the hidden talents of soldiers. Maybe it's my innate view that every person on the planet, regardless of social status, race, age, gender, or sexuality, has something to offer. Regardless of any existential factor, I had found another teacher.

To finish that investing story, I analysed my results over the subsequent year and noticed I was becoming better able to sustain profits. I was investing in my own niche, and it worked. This was a seismic change. My original vision was starting to become a reality. The point here for *Decision Point* readers is my lesson about where to find teachers. In the first example, it was from a superior, and in the second case, it was from one of my employees.

This experience has been incredibly powerful for me over the years. It has emphasised my need to keep a very open mind to where who and what form my next lesson will come from, be that traditionally in somebody I want to emulate or non-traditionally and any other opportunity to learn something new.

I wanted to share these experiences with you in the hope that you can find some inspiration in your own journey in achieving your goals. There are countless numbers of people who can help you if you open your mind becoming a student and broaden your search in looking for a teacher. You sometimes don't have to look too far for those teachers. When I look at children and teenagers today, their ability to exploit technology, apps, social media, and even the TV in the house far surpasses anyone from my generation. Don't discriminate because of age, gender, opinion, or social status. There's often a lot to learn from other people's viewpoints. You have a lot to learn, and everybody will teach you something if you're accepting of it.

CHAPTER 7

A Journey to Success

If you can't fly, then run. If you can't run, then walk. If
you can't walk then crawl, but by all means, keep moving.
—Dr. Martin Luther King

For *Decision Point* to demonstrate its guiding principles, I have been
fortunate enough to interview successful individuals who have pursued
their own goals against all odds and experienced similar obstacles, but all
shared the same passion. I used a set of eleven questions listed below to
present their success journey explicit, but I'd like for you to look for the
hidden message in each of the interviews! If you don't get it by the end of
the chapter, you'll know by the end of the book.

David Hogg, Start-up Entrepreneur, Mobile Gym Fitness

**What is your earliest memory of either thinking differently or wanting
to do something different?**

I worked in the fitness industry from the age of seventeen, starting
as a leisure attendant in my local health and fitness centre, on the
Youth Training Scheme. This was a 1980s policy where the government
introduced a practical and hands-on alternative for school leavers aged
between sixteen and seventeen in an effort to curb riots that had gone on
earlier in the decade.

During the 1980s, unemployment was high, jobs were scarce, and university wasn't even a consideration because of the wealth divide at the time. The Youth Training Scheme, or YTS as it became known, spanned multiple industries. I was already fit and active at school so the thought of working in a gym really attracted me. I remember my first day when five of us turned up at the gym, not really knowing what to expect, but in the same breath we probably had visions of pumping iron and staring into a mirror admiring our work.

Time passed as it does, and after a slight promotion from making cups of tea and emptying bins, we were presented with opportunities to develop. This included anything from shadowing a senior member of staff, sitting in a meeting and taking notes, or even going on a training course, but the single biggest impact for me was finding a mentor.

At the time of course the sixteen-year-old David didn't see these tasks as opportunities or anything more significant than one of the team asking me to help out, but on reflection, I can see that being exposed to something slightly different and outside of my comfort zone was hugely important in giving me the foundations to help me become the person I am today.

Life in the gym was different from what I had initially expected when I started on the YTS. There was a lot more paperwork and meetings, but because it was all related to what I had discovered was my real passion in life, I didn't mind. Two years later, my YTS scheme had finished and had served its purpose because I wanted to be a fitness professional. I stayed on at the health and fitness centre and really thrived in the environment. I was starting to become known and even started to work my way up the ladder, from leisure attendant to health and fitness manager in only a few years. At this point, I had my earliest memory of thinking differently or wanting to do something different.

My first day as the health and fitness manager, the general manager asked for my professional opinion on which fitness equipment should be installed in our new gym. I felt for the first time that I could make a real difference to this business, my ideas could give our members a better experience, and our gym could generate more money at the same time. I now had a team of people working for me, and it was my role to manage and develop my team to reach our new targets.

Why did you want to do or be something different?

The fitness industry is massive and constantly changing, whether it is a new type of training or kooky type of diet. Twenty years ago, the approach to strength and conditioning was totally different from what it is today. Back then, strength was all about strapping on the biggest weights on a bar you possibly could and lifting to failure, but today there are CrossFit athletes who never lift heavy weights or gymnasts who, pound for pound, are probably the strongest people in the industry.

And as for conditioning, back in the 1990s, I don't think it was even in the vernacular of the fitness industry. You either did strength or cardio. I like the changing nature of the fitness industry because its constant change is all geared toward improving human performance for all ages, so because the industry is changing, you have to change and try to think outside of the box. I found that several times I came up with an innovative idea, I would write it down but not take any action. Then lo and behold, I would discover that somebody else had the same idea but actually acted on it. I had so many great ideas in my head, but due to my dyslexia, I would find it difficult to go back to the ideas on paper and make sense of what I had written. This was so frustrating for me.

It was an innate drive to want to achieve, so I was always looking for solutions to any obstacles I was faced with. I think it was because of my constant searching for answers that I came across mind mapping, which, for me, was a great way to put my vision down on paper. So when it came to recalling those notes, I actually understood that flash thought or vision and was able to grow it. I used this method for one or two of my smaller projects, and it worked well, bringing the team together and, more importantly, giving me more confidence in my own ability. I then used mind mapping to start my most successful idea, developing a business where I could take the gym to a client's house!

After personal training for a number of years, I never felt I was giving true value to my home visit personal training clients because I was only bringing a selective amount of equipment to their house and charging a premium price. Not only that, when I got to my clients' homes, we would spend five minutes either side of the training session moving furniture around to make some space for the workout. I wanted to do better and to add more value. My idea of bringing a fully air-conditioned gym with the latest fitness equipment was something that had never been offered in the fitness industry before, and I wanted to make it possible.

And the more I spoke to people about the dream, the more motivated I was to make the dream happen. I can tell you now that I didn't get all positive responses. There were a lot of critics and negative responses, which, being honest, really knocked my confidence. This criticism did affect me, but now I had this idea, it wouldn't go away. I knew I would be letting myself down if I didn't act on this idea after I had let go of so many others. I realised I had to turn the negatives to positives and keep chasing the dream.

What decisions have been the most difficult for you?

When starting up any business, you face several difficult decisions, and in any start-ups I've been involved in, I've always found the initial financial decisions most difficult. Starting a business can appear to be a really selfish endeavour; you have this vision for this project. While everything I do is geared toward improving the lives of other people and my family, starting a business doesn't appear to show that from the outset. The financial decisions and commitment of capital and funding are you saying, "I want to start this business. I believe it's going to work. In fact, it has to work. And I believe it so much I'm going to borrow money from a bank to make it work."

There are no safety nets here. No insurance company will bail you out, so when I take financial decisions, they are really important to me, as they should be for any entrepreneur. I am a family man, and my financial decisions (which, I should add, I do speak to my wife about) affect my family as all entrepreneurs' decisions affect their loved ones. So to improve the chances of making the right decisions, I used a mentor, and now I have forty years of business experience an email away.

Another reason is that I am highly passionate about anything I get involved in, and I have learnt that you need to take a step back sometimes and look at your business idea or project from a different angle to achieve success. When it comes to committing to any financial decisions, you need to calculate the risk against the reward and, most importantly, what is affordable. This, for me, is where I found critics quite useful. They are always there, and it may even surprise you whom they turn out to be, but the service they provide is to pick holes in your business before, during, and after you launch your business. So when I have a big financial decision to make, I always speak to friends, colleagues, other business owners, and my mentor to critique my thoughts.

Who has influenced your decisions?

Family, friends, and clients have all influenced me in decisions I have ever made in business. Talking to as many people as possible allows you to pitch your idea to another of different audiences with a difference of opinions. I am fortunate. I have a really supportive family who trust me and believe in me. This just adds fuel to my fire and is why I get up in the morning. I also have a strong group of friends who are all of similar mind and entrepreneurial spirit in their own right, so getting support for Mobile Gym Fitness has been easy. But interestingly enough, my professional group and client group is where the most diversity in opinion came from.

In the gym where I worked, a small percentage of colleagues said Mobile Gym Fitness wouldn't work, that clients came to the gym for a social experience and to use all of the facilities. I knew this demographic of client was already in the gym, but from my research, they weren't my target market. So I went back to thinking outside of the box. I knew there were a large group of people out there who would really enjoy and benefit from personal training but were either too self-conscious to go to a gym or couldn't afford the high annual membership fees that gyms have to charge to pay for all of those facilities.

This was my target, and this was the group of people I wanted to help. So two years later, Mobile Gym is the UK's fastest-growing fitness franchise! I couldn't keep up with demand, so speaking to my mentor and my support group, we decided it was perfect for franchising and therefore could support more people across the country. It's been the most amazing journey, so my influences have been both positive and negative, but each time it's been my main job to understand the influence and use it to help me to make the right decisions. The more you talk about your idea, the more it helps you bring your visions to life and highlight potential hurdles that will need to be addressed along the way.

Did you consciously want to be the best at what you do?

I have always loved keeping fit and active and wanted to help get the most out of people. So being the best at what I do is so important to me, as my success is other people's success, and the more people I can serve and help in achieving their goals, the better. I'm not looking to dominate the world with Mobile Gym Fitness, but I do want to give 100 per cent to what I do, and as Mobile Gym Fitness is my vision, I want that to be 100 per cent too. So I discipline myself to always look the part. It's important for me to look like a fitness professional and for me to be able to demonstrate techniques and give advice. The kit and equipment used by my clients are the best and most fit for purpose I can find. This is a challenge at times because those items may be very very expensive, and for any start-up entrepreneur, cash is the lifeblood of the business. So you can't go spending all of your money without considering how that expenditure will impact on the whole business.

All Mobile Gym Fitness vans are spotlessly clean for all clients, and following some critique during my planning stages, they have to smell very clean for each client. So you get the idea, these, among others, are some of the ideas and rules I have implemented into helping my franchisees maintain my Mobile Gym Fitness brand and to support them in building their own businesses.

A technique I was taught when setting myself goals so I could maximise my potential and my outputs was to work in a SMART way. It's fairly well known in the management world, but from what I have found, it's not widely known or used outside of the project management world. SMART stands for Specific, Measurable, Achievable, Realistic, Timeframe.

So when I set up Mobile Gym Fitness, I would set weekly and monthly goals that I could see if I achieved them or not. I used specific targets to make sure the business was properly set up as a legal and trading entity, so this meant lots of support from my mentor and his business team and a pretty steep learning curve. Once I had set those specific goals, each week

I would write a report feeding back to my mentor on the progress I had made. This was good for two reasons:

1. I got to track the progress of Mobile Gym Fitness's creation.
2. I was holding myself to account by drilling down into what I had actually achieved and if I had listened to and followed the advice of my mentor.

My mentor helped me with the next two aspects of my SMART targets and goal setting because while I had grand visions of launching the business locally initially, I had already started to plan my national and international expansion. Ambition is good, and all entrepreneurs have this in abundance, but in the early stages of business development, the short-term goals have to be achievable and realistic because nobody believes in your business or product more than you. So it's strange and a bit frustrating when you have to sell the idea to other people. (He said this with a smile on his face.) Finally those goals and objectives I had set myself had to be wrapped in a sensible time frame.

You never really know how long it will take for a business to succeed. I suppose that depends on what business success looks like for each individual, but in any case, having a time frame or even multiple time frames such as short, medium, and long term will help you measure that success. This method of goal setting applies to any field or speciality, and I would recommend it to anybody.

Is what you do an effort?

Being in a job you love doesn't require any effort, and to me, this is my measure of success. A lot of people look at your financial outcomes as a level of success, but for me, it's about having good health, being surrounded by positive people, and getting 100 per cent satisfaction and enjoyment out of everything you do. Having a positive mindset will help achieve a positive outcome. I go to bed each night looking forward to the next day because of knowing that what I have planned is going to take me one more step forward in growing Mobile Gym Fitness and also the not knowing what opportunities or new people I meet will present themselves. I am always open to this and learning every day. I think if more people pursued happiness rather than wealth, the world would be a better place.

Would you rather do something else?

I have had several different interests in other types of jobs but have always had a strong belief that the fitness industry was an industry that needed my skillset. It is an industry that I fully understand and can make a difference in, for both fitness professionals and end users. And like I said, it's where I have always found happiness. Knowing I have the potential to transform the fitness industry tells me that there is nothing else that I would rather do.

How did you stay motivated through tough times?

Let me tell you: in business, you will be faced with some really tough times, and you will feel like giving up! However, if you surround yourself with positive people and are not afraid to ask for help, be prepared for and don't be surprised if you make some wrong decisions. That will ultimately make you a stronger and wiser person for the next time you are presented with a new problem. You will be able to deal with bigger and more complex issues, and knowing that for each decision, good and bad, will ultimately benefit Mobile Gym Fitness. This keeps me motivated during those tough times.

What disciplines did you employ to achieve the success you have?

What I find, and I think it's similar for most people, is that the things you least like doing, you will put on the back-burner. You know, "I'll get round to doing that tomorrow or next week and so on." Take doing your accounts or doing paperwork. That's really not something that motivates me. I want to be out promoting Mobile Gym Fitness, growing the client base, and supporting my franchisees. So the disciplines I try to employ are to do those things first, and once they are out of the way, everything else will be more enjoyable and easier to do. Second, I use my SMART objectives to give me a plan of action each week, so at the end of the week I review if I have achieved those objectives. After all, I created them because they were necessary to grow the business and for my own happiness.

Finally with those SMART objectives, my targets are small and achievable. It's a lot of little steps that have gotten Mobile Gym Fitness to where it is today, and I believe it will be lots of little steps that will take it to the next level.

Does it ever get easier?

I wouldn't say it ever gets easier. I would say you would find better ways of doing things to achieve your outcomes. There will always be hurdles, problems, and difficult times that will require your attention. But as time goes by, you will create new tools, methods, and contacts that will help you to overcome these problems. In Mobile Gym Fitness, the first problems I came across were funding and how to get financial backing to support my vision. When I overcame this problem, then it was a case of converting the vehicles in the most modular and cost-efficient way to give my clients and franchisees the best experience and real value for money at the same time as being a profitable business. Then the problems associated with scale had to be dealt with, so you see the problems are always there. I see them as a good thing because it means you are growing and not stagnant. I think it's part and parcel of being an entrepreneur.

What are your top-five tips for *Decision Point* readers?

First, for change to happen, change has to occur! What I mean: if you keep doing what you are doing, you will never reach new goals. In life, you need to have direction, and if you keep following the same pathway, you will end up at that destination. If you want to explore new outcomes, you will have to think about walking down a different path.

Second, always complete the tasks you least like doing first. Third, have belief in yourself and don't be afraid to ask for help when you need it. Fourth, surround yourself with positive people, embrace negativity, and turn it into a positive when you can. Finally, be SMART when setting your goals.

Paul Hardcastle, Chart-topping music artist

What is your earliest memory of either thinking differently or wanting to do something different?

I hated school. I used to be the disruptive kid in the class because I didn't want to be there. I just wasn't interested. I think I was about fourteen when I was introduced to motorbikes. All my mates had motorbikes, and they let me have a go round the blocks of flats near where we lived, and I think I had, not so much a gift, but I just wasn't afraid of taking risks.

So my first thoughts were that I wanted to be a motorbike racer rather than going to a maths class, and this led to me thinking that school was an even worse thing for me to do. I was totally addicted to motorbikes, and that was the first thing I actually wanted to do as a profession, so that became my first job when I left school, and I left school early.

I got myself a little job as a dispatch rider for £12 per week, just delivering prints because obviously there was no internet, faxes, or that sort of stuff then, so if someone had something they wanted printing and they needed to see a proof of it, it would need to be biked over to them. Then they would say, "OK, go and print that."

So that was the first time that I thought, "I love this."

I would do it in the wet. I would take jobs that no one wanted to do because I loved driving motorbikes, and that was my first thoughts of a career I wanted to do.

Why did you want to do or be something different?

My dad was a jazz musician, and when I was eight, he taught me to play the guitar and drums. I used to go all around Europe with him. I would come on halfway through the show, and people would be quite amazed because I was this young kid who could play a couple instruments. We were never living in one place, so I guess I was different from that sort of era because I never had a steady home life. It was more a question of where are we going now, so that was normal for me.

What decisions have been the most difficult for you?

Leaving my job. I'd just gotten a mortgage with my girlfriend, and I thought that I couldn't do both at the same time. So I took the risk that I would do OK. I guess it was faith in myself, and it was difficult because if music had gone wrong, then I don't know what would have happened. I had faith in myself, and I was very lucky that the first track I did when we got the mortgage sold 500,000 records for my first Paul Hardcastle record. And that was like … Whoa. So the difficulty was taking the risk, leaving my job, and having a belief in myself.

"19" wasn't my first big hit. My first big hit was a track called "Rainforest," which went to number one on the R&B chart in America, and that's how I got to meet Simon Fuller. He called me up because "Rainforest" happened to knock Madonna off the top of the twelve-inch sales chart, so he invited me in for a chat.

It was really fun. He asked if there were anything else I was working on, which I was. I happened to be working on "19." I took it in and played it to the hierarchy of Chrysalis Records. And when I played it, they looked at me like I was an alien. Seriously! But remember this was something totally different, and they had never heard N,N,N,N (all of the stuttering). I had come up with something that was crazy, and I felt like shrinking.

But there were a couple guys who had faith in it. One was Simon Fuller; the other was my promoter, who said this was either going to be great or rubbish. They all said it would never get played on radio, but as it transpired, it was the biggest record played on the radio for two months. So when you're asking about decisions, I made the decision to say to them, "If you don't like this record, then I'll take it somewhere else."

Who has influenced your decisions?

Simon Fuller was very influential in what I was doing. There were certain things he said I should and shouldn't do. There was a record just after "19" called "19 not out" by a guy called Rory Bremner, and it was a parody of "19." It was all about cricket, and my record company said, "No, you can't get involved in this, Paul. You've just made this big, bold political statement. You can't now do something funny," but I said, "If I can't make fun out of myself, then I'm not as good a person that I think I am."

Dave Gilmour from Pink Floyd was also a big influence for me. We had a good chat, and I said, "You don't really play fast, do ya, Dave?"

He said, "No, I've never wanted to be a fast player, but people remember what I play."

And that for me was like, "Hey, it's really about doing what's right for you." That worked out really well for me when I did "Rainforest."

Did you consciously want to be the best at what you do?

I didn't have a clue what was going to happen. I just love making music.

Is what you do an effort?

No, not in any shape or form. I have been very lucky because my audience has stuck with me ever since "Rainforest." My last album (thirty years on after "19") has had four number ones from it, and the audience I have gotten has been absolutely fantastic. I have worked out of every album I've put out, I've had at least one number-one single from it. So I've had at least twenty-eight or thirty number ones on the R&B, Jazz chart on Billboard in America, or the Smooth Jazz chart, so it's been fantastic, and I have this great relationship with my audience, so it's not an effort at all.

Although I didn't start with music, it's always been with me. I had a motorcycle accident earlier in my life, which stopped any thoughts of a career in racing, but because of that, I spend a lot of time in bed listening to the radio. I recognised some of the music and the beats from when I used to tour with my dad, so I wondered if I could get back into it. I bought a monophonic keyboard, which could only play one note at a time, but I had this idea that if I got two cassette decks, I could record one note and then bounce. It would be two notes and bounce it back, and it would be a chord. Unfortunately it sounded like frying in a chip shop. The hiss that came from it was crazy.

So that was my first entry into music. I started coming up with some ideas and looked around in *Melody Maker*, a local music newspaper, and saw an ad saying "keyboard player wanted."

I thought, "It's not going to work, but I'll give it a try."

They had this pianist who blew me off the planet, so I thought to myself that I might as well walk out, but because of the type of music I was doing (funk) and this other guy being more classically trained, they asked me if I'd like to join the band.

Now I thought, "Hang on a minute. Is it April 1 because I'm entirely self-taught?"

But they said, "No, you will suit our band better."

And this showed me then that you don't have to be classically trained to fit into a certain genre. And I was like "Wow," so I joined the band, and it went on from there. There are people in America who are miles more talented than I am, but the only thing they can't do is write great melodies that people want to listen to. That's where I really excel. I make music for my audience, not just to show how fast I can play or to make money.

Would you rather do something else?

Yes, being a motorbike racer or a footballer. I played in a celebrity tournament called the celebrity soccer six, and I played with some of the top players in the world, all for charity. And I remember scoring my first goal at Chelsea, and the rush I got from seeing the ball hit the back of the net is more instantaneous than getting a number one.

How did you stay motivated through tough times?

This might sound awful, but I don't think I've had many tough years. The reason why is because I've been motivated to give people the best, and I mean the best I can give. There might be times where I've mixed something over a month or so, and I've thought at the end, "I can get this better, and my fans deserve the best I can actually give."

For example, some footballers give the best they can all of the time, and others don't. Some of them are lazy, and it's just for the money. I never got into music thinking I could make a living from it, and when you start from that mindset, the music is purer. I just did it because I loved what I was doing, and when you love what you're doing, it just works.

What disciplines did you employ to achieve the success you have?

Being true to myself and not compromising has been important to me. Because I'm not motivated by money, my biggest discipline now is making sure I give my fans the best music I can, no matter how long it takes.

Does it ever get easier?

It is harder now. Now I have made over thirty albums because I don't want to keep on repeating myself, and unfortunately when you're a musician, there's a certain way you do things. If you heard a Beatles record, everyone would know it's the Beatles. So for me, everyone knows if it's a Paul Hardcastle record, so I try and reinvent myself. So I change from Hardcastle 1-8, and I've done "the Chill lounge," which is more Ibiza-type sounds. But the good thing is that all of my audience has followed wherever I have gone. They get it.

There's a track I did with my daughter, Maxine Hardcastle, called "Where I wanna be," and you will see that it's nothing like what I normally do, but it has my daughter on it. It's like a chilled dance record. I do change what I do, so it's easier to produce music technically, but it is not easy to make a better record than what I have previously done. So it's a constant challenge.

What are your top five tips for *Decision Point* readers?

First, if you believe in yourself, then don't listen to anyone else. Just go for it. Second, life is hard, and sometimes you can't always pick the things you want to do. So if you have to go to work to support someone, then you can do two hours a week at college or something that gets you to where you want to be. Use the internet and forums to help you to do what you want to do. There's so much knowledge out there, but pick and choose the advice. Third is discipline. It's a big thing. I used to go into the studio for fifteen hours a day because of point one. Fourth, you have to be happy. Don't compare yourself with anyone else. I've met people with everything, and it's still not enough. You get one life, so enjoy it. I don't think you need a fifth if you get those four right.

Glen Rowe, Tour manager for the rock band, Muse, for over eighteen years

What is your earliest memory of either thinking differently or wanting to do something different?

Well, I have quite a funny upbringing really. My dad was an ex-professional wrestler, and my mum was a florist. My dad was from Skinningrove in Yorkshire, a real poor miners' town near Whitby on that coast. Skinningrove was literally just a miners' town, so in the 1980s when they started to close the mines, it fell into massive decay. My mother was an only child and daughter to a cleaner who worked and cleaned in Windsor Castle, so somehow this northern and southern division met in a pub in Old Windsor playing darts one night. So while my dad was a professional wrestler, he was also a builder because unlike today, wrestlers weren't making enough money back in the 1960s and 1970s to make a living. My dad then went to South Africa on a wrestling tour to try to promote wrestling and export it as a new sport, in the same way we have had American football games here in London or how we are now exporting British football [soccer] to the U.S.

So on this tour, my dad fell head over heels in love with the place and ended up moving there permanently, and Mum and Dad lived there for five years. I was actually born in South Africa, where I lived until I was three years old before coming back to London. By the time we came back to the UK, my dad had almost retired from wrestling but was still in the building trade. Looking back, I remember that my upbringing was on a council estate, classic dad builder and mum with an artistic flair, being a florist.

My earliest memory of wanting to be something different was getting up at four o'clock in the morning in Mum's little red van, driving to the flower market in Western International and watching her do business, and my mum was genius in her way of getting the best deals from anybody. I remember being amazed just watching her hustle, so after the flower market, it was back to the shop where I had to fill up buckets of water for the flowers. I recall how important these flowers were because we had just paid for them, so if I damaged them, we would lose money.

I remember thinking, "This is what it's like to run your own business." That energy that she didn't have to report to anybody was quite amazing. At that point, something clicked.

I don't know exactly what, but I realised that there are two kinds of people on Planet Earth, those who follow their pension packet and those who follow their passion. So my dad was fully subscribed to getting a pension, and my mum followed her passion. So those two ways of thinking were very different, and I guess I just gravitated toward my mum's way of thinking and her ideology that if you love what you do for work, you don't feel like you're working.

Why did you want to do or be something different?

I feel really privileged that I discovered when I was really young that working can be brilliant and doesn't have to be a chore. You don't have to come home and say, "I had a terrible day at work." I mean, my wife gets annoyed because she'll ask me how my day was, and every day, I'll say to her, "Fucking brilliant! I had a great day at work!"

I love it. I'm now forty-six years old, and I don't feel like I've been to work yet, but I've worked really hard. I've packed in two or three careers worth of hard work during that time, but I've genuinely loved it.

What decisions have been the most difficult for you?

Not going to university was a big one, which might surprise you because I really didn't enjoy school, but the attraction for me wasn't academia. It was because a few of my mates had headed off to university and had this carefree lifestyle. I also dropped out of art school because I was in a band and we had been given the opportunity to go on tour. The college wouldn't allow me to take time off my course to go on this tour, so I just had to quit to go and be a drummer in a band. I had a lot more fun doing that anyway.

So I have two brothers. I'm the youngest of three. My oldest brother was a daydreamer, and my middle brother was a hooligan [chuckles]. I would play the drums in my garage as a kid and have a desire to get away from there. I dreamed of higher things, and I didn't want to be like everyone else. I can distinctly remember friends at the time laughing at me for growing my hair long, which for me was normal because I wanted to be in a rock band.

So for me, it was a need to be different, and I had the benefit of seeing my entire future through my father and my two older brothers, who were hitting the same pubs and hanging out with their mates. My mum was the ultimate cheerleader for me, and she would say, "You can do whatever you want to do. Go and do it! Don't let anything stop you. Just keep going." And that would give me so much confidence. She would say, "There are drains and radiators in a room. Are you someone who warms up the room or someone who sucks the life out of it?"

I always wanted to be different, and I remember a few things. Breakdancing in the 1980s was the first stage of me daring to be different. Then I wanted to play baseball because I fell in love with American culture, and I was the only boy in the Cobham Yankees who was from England. They were puzzled, saying things like, "Who is this Brit guy?" All of my friends would ask me why I wasn't playing football with the rest of them, and I'd be thinking, "I don't want to be like the rest of you."

I just couldn't fit in. I didn't want to. I like difference. I have always been a little bit anarchic, a little bit punk. I like the quirky people and those who dare to dream because they're the ones who do great things.

Later on in life, I would discover that I was a little bit different anyway. Not being very academic, I found out that I had both OCD and ADHD, but rather than consider this a negative thing, I embraced it and learned to really enjoy it. Creatives aren't usually very academic so they are compelled into other walks of life. I think schools have got it wrong. Schools want you to fit into shapes and boxes, but life isn't like that, and the world needs a bit of everything.

So the difficulty for me was separating myself from my family. At that point, I really did pull away. I split up with my girlfriend, stopped being in the band I was in, booked a flight to America, and travelled around on my own. I wanted to recharge. I think it's really cathartic to think about it like a snake shedding its skin. That was one part of my life, and I was about to emerge and create a new future for my life. So breaking away from the commonality and norms of where I grew up was huge.

Who has influenced your decisions?

My mum was a massive influence for me, but so was my father because he showed me something I didn't want to be. So as much as a pedestal I put my mum on, my father was equally influential. He was the yang to her yin, and all of my experiences growing up, good and bad, have shaped who I am today.

It's hard to compartmentalise your emotions sometimes because I do think that you should be able to lock those feelings in boxes and forget about them. Sometimes that's actually what you need, or it certainly has been my coping strategy for all these years. I would say to myself, "You know what? I don't want to think like that anymore. Are these thoughts helping me move forward or backward?"

My decisions are mine, and I own them. I don't look back to bad examples from my dad as some sort of excuse for not making a decision or making the wrong one. That wouldn't be positive or help me progress in the things I do and with the people I meet. Outside of my immediate family, my friends' parents influenced me. I had a broad selection of friends who all had great parents. I admired the family values they lived, and that has stayed with me to now, where I try to be the best for my own children.

Did you consciously want to be the best at what you do?

Yes. I wanted to be the best drummer in my school, and when I achieved that, I then wanted to be the best drummer in my college. Then I wanted to be the best drummer in the area. So bit by bit, I was growing in confidence. I always had this attitude, even though I was acting locally, I was thinking globally. I wanted to be in the best band so I would take charge of the art, band management, and the business side of the music, and that has never changed. I still want to be the best drummer [chuckle]. I still want to be the best son, best brother, best father, and best husband I can be.

What's also important for me is that I know I'm probably not going to be the best at all of those things. That's a lot of pressure to try to be all you can be for so many different people, but it doesn't stop me from trying.

Is what you do an effort?

No, not at all.

Would you rather do something else?

Absolutely not.

How did you stay motivated through tough times?

The tough times are when you are challenged the most, and I've always looked at that thinking the bad days make the good days better, so I try to think positively and keep on going because the sun will shine again tomorrow.

Something so simple happened in my life that changed my perspective. I attended a scuba diving course to get my PADI qualification, and I wanted to go on to do fifty dives to get my divemaster qualification.

So I was in Australia with my brothers. We'd been drinking a lot and going diving. (And you're not supposed to do that, by the way.) And by the end of this particular dive session we were doing, I was absolutely exhausted, but I forced myself out of bed because later that day we were doing a drift dive, where you're dropped off at a particular point and have to make your own way back. It's dangerous. Drift diving carries with it more inherent risks than conventional diving. So we all get in the water, and I feel bad. I know I feel bad and probably shouldn't continue with the dive, but I do anyway. Before I knew it, a rip starts pulling me toward the rocks, and I'm about twenty meters down, which is so many atmospheres more pressure than the surface.

I really had to stay calm. I noticed I was using more air than normal because I was tired and wasn't kicking very well, so I started to get a bit worried because a quick appraisal of the situation suggested to me that I was probably not going to make it back to the surface.

I was looking around in a slight panic, and I saw a school of fish, with one in particular looking me right in the eyes, and I thought to myself, "Oh, that's what you're supposed to be doing."

What the fish was doing was moving with the current, so when the current was against it, the fish would go limp and flow with the wave. And when the current moved in the opposite direction, the direction the fish wanted to swim, the fish would swim with all its might to move forward, and it made marginal gains, little bits at a time.

And I thought to myself, "That is the answer to my life. When everything is going against you, don't fight it. Go with it and let it push you around sometime. And then when you're ready, you give it everything you've got." And that philosophy got me out of trouble that day when in Australia and it has gotten me out of trouble countless times since, all because of a little fish. Marginal gains in life motivate me to keep going when it gets tough.

What disciplines did you employ to achieve the success you have?

Self-belief has been the foundation for me and knowing that when the time comes, to give it all I have.

Does it ever get easier?

No, don't think it does. But that's not because the tasks never get harder. It's because I continue to push myself to continually keep my goals and standards high. My desire and drive are still the same as it was when I was an eleven-year-old boy, to when I was managing Muse and touring the world, and now as I have launched the UK's number-one record label for up and coming artists in Kyoto Music. I won't be happy until it's perfect, but the funny thing is that I won't know when it's perfect. I say this to the acts I've managed over the years and those I manage now, "The day you think you've written the best song in your career, it's over," because you can never write your best song. I believe that is true in artist management, and I believe that business.

The thought of retirement scares me to death. As I'm getting older, it's becoming more present because people are talking about it now. I'm only forty-six! People ask me if I have a pension, and I say no. I want to die working, doing what I love. Why would you retire? Everything I've learned, I need to carry on doing and passing that on to others who can get something from it and create fantastic creative art. I don't think that sitting on a deck chair in paradise living out your days is an outdated concept for an outdated way of working. People don't leave school or university and then go and work for a single company until they retire. People are agile and full of energy, even if they aren't in the creative space. It's still normal for people to have three to five employers in their working lives. I think I'll always look for the next challenge.

What are your top five tips for *Decision Point* readers?

1. Don't let the bastards grind you down.
2. Listen, learn, and lead. You've always got something to learn. I'll listen to everyone's opinion, but then I'll make my own mind up. I'm in a really fortunate position where through my charity, I get to speak to young teenagers about the music industry. And I tell them the same thing: it's all about passion; you can achieve anything you want as long as you really are passionate about it. And if you want to be an accountant, be the best accountant you can be and don't limit yourself to an office in the city somewhere. You can be a tour accountant in the music industry, you can be an army accountant, or you can be an accountant in Formula One. So whatever you love, find the most exciting way you can to present that.
3. Travel. I know it's a cliché, but travel really does completely change everything. If you don't see other languages, colours, tastes, and music from different parts of the world, you haven't lived. We are very lucky now that travel is more accessible and can be inexpensive.
4. Don't worry. Just follow your heart and don't let anyone take you off track. There's a reason why racehorses wear blinkers. It's to stop them from being distracted by what's going on around them so they can focus on going forward toward the finish line. Rocket ships don't have rearview mirrors. Nobody cares what's back there. It's all about the goal.
5. Get out of your comfort zone. This is where you are alive. This is where you'll be pushed, stretched, and rewarded with all of life's gifts. I am a normal guy with a poor- to middle-class upbringing, and I'm not the sharpest, but if I can do it, anyone can do it.

Anna Stephens, ex-Army officer and entrepreneur, founder of Anna-Motion Fitness and Mum

What is your earliest memory of either thinking differently or wanting to do something different?

I applied for the army at the age of fifteen. I joined the cadets at school. I did a few camps, and I just loved it. I was a bossy kid, and I liked telling people what to do. So I was put in charge of other people, and that went well. So then I was allowed to be in charge of lots of people. And I found that the more people I was in charge of, the more I loved it. It was physically challenging and so different from anything else that I had experienced. I just flew. My mom could see how much I was enjoying it and said I could apply for a scholarship with the army.

So I applied and had to go through the selection process, which as far as I could see was just more fun. After that process had run its course, I finally got my place at the Royal Military Academy Sandhurst when I was sixteen. I was a very confident young girl, and in the army if you show just a spark of interest for leadership, motivation, sport, or, I guess, anything, it will take you and allow you to go forward to be the best you can be. I didn't think I was at all unusual because I found myself in an environment where I was usually one of the only girls. That never really bothered me, and I didn't find the army a particularly sexist place. It was fun, and I fit into army life seamlessly. It felt like a natural decision.

Why did you want to do or be something different?

Leaving the army felt like a big decision, but I absolutely had to do it. I was exhausted. And I think it's a symptom of the army constantly pushing you because you change jobs every two to three years. So you have a new job every two to three years, and you approach it with the same energy, always pushing yourself. The thing you sacrifice is your health, your family, and your others. You have no other life in the army it's just the army. Life is fun. Don't get me wrong. It's not like it's a bad thing, but it's so selfish. You go on exercises, you're constantly away, you talk about yourself, and the house is all about and you. I've got two children. And they are at an age where they just say, "Can you just be a normal mom?" So I realized I really wasn't normal. I really wasn't. I was committed to my work, and I was leading a very selfish life.

I read this post on social media, and somebody had used this exercise to evaluate where you are in life. You take a piece of paper and list all the things important to you on one side (one, two, and three) and then write how much time you allocate to each of those things. So of course I put children and husband, and I realised the army didn't feature at all. And then on the righthand side, I saw that I literally had spent no time with them because I was on exercise overseas and doing army things. I had managed to speak to them on the phone if I were lucky.

The post went on to say that if you only slightly match, then maybe you've got it wrong. It really hit home, and I suddenly thought that if I don't do something about this now, my life is just going to pass me by, my children are just going to leave home, and I am going to be gutted because I won't have had that time with them that I really want to have. And I don't necessarily know them as well as I think I do; it was a big wake-up call.

On leaving, I did look for jobs, but whenever I came to a particular question on an application form, "Why do you want this job?" I couldn't answer it because I didn't want it at all. I felt so free, empowered, and liberated from leaving the military. I felt like I got my freedom back. So starting my own business was incredible because it was mine and I could do what I wanted with it. Having that freedom to say how many clients I'm going to have, what days I'm going to work, and which classes I'm going to do, what do I love? I'm just going to do what I love. And I felt alive again, completely alive by that thing that everybody says, "You find a job you love, and you don't feel like you're working." That's me. Now that is literally me.

What decisions have been the most difficult for you?

It's priorities. It still is making sure that my priorities are always in check. But the hardest decisions I'm having to make now is making sure that I don't grow too fast so the work doesn't overwhelm me. I've been fortunate enough to have an abundance of clients. I was literally doing back-to-back classes, and I found I can very quickly get into that state I was in when I was in the army, that I'd become too busy and start to stress. So it took action to rein it back in.

I don't think I've felt this well and healthy since I was in my twenties because I make sure I look after myself, and a lot of that is I allow myself to do frivolous things. I allow myself to just chill. I read books. I walk the dog for forty minutes every day. I'm the dullest person, but I'm so happy. And that's the thing I think you go to again. It's that list. What makes you happy? How long do you spend doing it?

So it's a bit like saying to yourself that you know what you love doing, so then you allow yourself to do it instead of thinking you're a terrible person for doing it. If it's what you want to do, do it, but manage it. So set a timer but don't beat yourself up for doing something you enjoy doing. It doesn't have to be worthy. It can be doing a jigsaw, gardening, or who cares. It doesn't matter. Just whatever it is you love, just be honest with yourself, and don't then feel bad about the fact you've done it. Otherwise what's the point of living if you're not doing anything you enjoy?

Who's influenced your decisions?

My parents, to begin with, were very supportive. They've always had my back, and always they knew me well enough and knew I was ambitious and had goals. My next big influence was when I left the military. When I was on my physical training course, the guy who ran the course was pretty good because he introduced me to coaching. And coaching has changed my mindset entirely because before I did the course, my understanding of coaching and mentoring had come from the army, but it wasn't as structured as to what I was now being exposed to. And so he introduced me to coaching on a much deeper and intellectual level, which was totally life-changing.

So I've learned not to tell people what to do. You can't tell people. You can't give them your motivation because everyone knows what they're supposed to do. You have to wait for them to say why they're not doing it, how are they going to improve, and what's going to keep them on track. And you just have to just wait because if they hear it coming out of their mouth, it's way more powerful than somebody else preaching to them.

Did you consciously want to be the best at what you do?

I'm horribly competitive. One of my clients (and now friend) said she was going to do a triathlon. I've never done one before, and this particular one was a mini sprint triathlon. I said, "Well, I'm not having you, my first client, go through a triathlon and then come back and say, "I've done a triathlon and you haven't done it. So I joined to do it with her. I had planned to swim with her, run with her … you get it … but as soon as that whistle blew, I was gone. I didn't see her again until the end. We laugh about it now. That is my competitive edge; that's my competitive spirit.

My thing is finding your own version of success. That's my whole deal. Like I said before, you know your version of being fit and strong, but as far as I'm concerned, I am honestly fitter and healthier than I have been in twenty years, and I feel fantastic about that. And that's what matters to me.

Is what you do an effort?

No, no, no. The biggest thing is not doing what I do. The kids know that my if I'm watching my screen, I'm watching some of the exercises my clients are doing, I'm watching my favourite people lift weights up and down, and it's my pleasure. It's not an effort at all. I love it.

Would you rather do something else?

No, I'm exactly where I want to be, doing exactly what I want to do, hanging out with the people I really want to be with. I have got my one-two-three spot from that list earlier.

How did you stay motivated through tough times?

It's not always easy working alone, as I've always been on a team of some description, and I've found that aspect tough, but I'm lucky to have people I can reach out to for advice and support. I am a fundamentally positive person, so that does help, but limiting thoughts do sneak in. I've accepted that there are aspects of my business that I am just not very good at or don't enjoy, so I'm happy to get help and ask others for advice. It's very freeing to just talk through your concerns and worries. The old adage of a problem shared is a problem halved is so very true in my experience.

What disciplines did you employ to achieve the success you have?

Be brave and network! You can have the best business in the world, but you need to tell people about it, and no one can do that better than you can as the business owner. So find a networking group. There are so many and get stuck in!

Does it ever get any easier?

Lots of things are easier. I don't worry about my programming anymore. I don't worry so much about the technical side of my job, whereas before I used to overthink and make sure I was absolutely right with my skills, drills, and techniques and building the program. I did spend a lot of time worrying about all that, but now that's all good. Things I need to do now is to grow the business and make it more profitable. That's going to be difficult because it's not something that comes naturally to me. It's not easy, things like sales and marketing and all the things I don't really know anything about. But I want to reach more people to have a bigger impact and to try to make my business more successful, so I need to do all of those things.

What are your top five tips for *Decision Point* readers?

I really enjoyed coming out with these because I write things down in my book all the time, stuff that really resonates. So first is to write a list because I think a lot of people aren't where they want to be in life, and then when you actually write a list and ask yourself, "What do I love doing?" What do you spend your time doing in order of priority? If they don't match, then maybe something has to change. I'm not saying it's easy because you have to earn money and you have to go out and get a job. But there are ways of getting those lists closer together. And that's really hard because you think then you've got to start planning, and I don't think most people plan.

Two, you can't out-train a bad diet. It's my favourite mantra, and I think this applies to anything in life. It doesn't matter how long you spend in the gym. You're not going to undo the fundamental thing that's wrong. If you are married to the wrong person, it doesn't matter what you do. You shouldn't be with that person. There are some fundamentals in life you need to make sure that are right. Don't fall into the trap of thinking you can do a quick fix for something that's fundamentally wrong. It's like holding that mirror up saying "I'm really unhappy" and asking yourself "Why am I unhappy?" Then be really honest with yourself about what's really wrong. And then you've got to do something that's probably going to be very hard for you to do.

Three, know what your version of success looks like and don't get distracted by shiny things (other people's version of success). So this is my other mantra of a kid who is on the podium with a silver medal. The gold medal-winning kid is grumpy for whatever reason. Perhaps they're used to winning, but the kid with the silver medal is literally having the best day of their life because they've never been on a podium before ever. That's their version of success, and they've made it. So your version of success is yours, literally nobody else's.

If a client of mine loses two pounds in a month, I'm going to celebrate that too. I'm going to make them feel like they're a million dollars because that is a massive success. Someone else may lose more, but it doesn't matter. If in your head you know what happy and success looks and feels like, no matter how long it takes to get there, you celebrate. You make sure you enjoy that feeling in that moment. Your goals have to be personal.

Four, be honest about what you're doing. This is where you should be try to be honest about who you are. If you are trying to pretend to be something that you're not, then let that go and just be true to you. And if you like doing crosswords and computer programming or fishing, then be that guy. Don't be the guy who goes to play football but secretly hates it. It's all about, "Are you doing the things you really enjoy or are you doing the things you think you should be doing and don't enjoy?"

Finally, be your biggest fan because no one else is going to be this for you. It's easily said, but if you're not backing yourself, you're not supporting you. Then that means you're relying on other people to do it, and everyone else is trying to get through their day. And everyone else is trying to find their own mojo. So you might be lucky. You might have a really great fan base. You might have lots of people who, like you, feel for them. Ultimately, if you want to achieve anything, you've got to accept you can't be second-guessing yourself and questioning your ability, inquiring whether you think you should or shouldn't. You've got to pump yourself up and just go for it.

Teri Ellington, Jewellery and watch entrepreneur[4]

What is your earliest memory of either thinking differently or wanting to do something different?

I think my earliest memory goes back to when I was a kid growing up. I was very much a tomboy. While my friends were into Barbie dolls, I was playing football, skateboarding, and doing things like that. So from that perspective, I always thought differently. But growing up from the age of around thirteen or fourteen, I was heavily influenced by acting and singing, which is where I found my passion. I had the opportunity to audition for a TV show on the BBC called *Wolf Blood*, so following the usual round of auditions when I was fourteen, I eventually got the part when I was fifteen. So from an early age, I've always known and felt that I wanted to and had to do something different. I had friends in school who were training to be solicitors and have career professions and that kind of thing, and I remember really clearly from a young age that I wanted something more than the ordinary.

Unfortunately when I was sixteen, I ended up struggling with mental health issues, which affected me massively for a couple years, and it was also at that point where I started having thoughts about what I was going to do with my life. Only a few years on from when I was twenty-one, I worked in a veterinary surgery as a kennel assistant, and I just kept having those thoughts, "What am I going to do?" I don't think I had the right mindset, and I thought the cards had been dealt for me. I ended up losing my job two months before Christmas, but it was the best thing that could have happened. I had always had an interest in fashion. I think that had

---

[4] www.ellingtontimepieces.com

come from entertainment and acting, and I just thought to myself that I was going to take the plunge.

I've always been a very creative person, so at twenty-one, I decided I was going to follow my passion and become a fashion designer, and that was how Ellington Timepiece was created. I was bullied at school. I used to tell myself that I was going to make something of my life, so pain for me was a motivator. I wanted to make a change. I wanted to prove other people wrong and to prove something to myself too.

Why did you want to do or be something different?

I always liked football, and I would play in the streets. I liked skateboarding and riding my bike, whereas other girl mates were more into dolls and things like that. And I think that might be an influence from my older brother. I had a younger sister, so I was the middle child. So I think that for me, I was just more of a tomboy. It wasn't until I went to high school where I really considered wearing makeup and doing my hair, so that's the point where my mindset really changed. Because I was bullied a little bit for being different.

I have always had a mentality that I want more from life and prove others wrong, and that also came from being bullied at school. My acting played a part in proving something to others because it was an escape for me. I've never wanted a normal life, and whether that meant travelling or meeting different people, but when I was sixteen, I felt like all of that went out of the window because I was struggling with mental health, which isn't something that ever goes away, but you just learn to cope and live with it a bit better. So now, my why has changed to me wanting to inspire people with my story and show the world my creations and my creativity.

What decisions have been the most difficult for you?

Decisions that were going to affect me in a big way. It's a lot easier to make those smaller day-to-day decisions I made in the early days of Ellington Timepiece, like whether or not to go to a promotion event or not, but when you make life-changing decisions, they weigh heavily. I remember deciding to go to London to audition for my part in *Wolf Blood* with the BBC, and I was a bag of nerves. I sat in the coffee shop outside the studio thinking all kinds of things like, "What if I don't get the part? What if I do get the part? It could change my life."

At fifteen years old, this felt like the biggest decision of my life, but as I've mentioned, I was successful in getting the part, which was a real confidence boost for me.

A bit later in life when I was twenty-one, I felt like I was at a crossroads again. I had £80 to my name and was deciding whether to become a self-employed entrepreneur. I had bills and responsibilities, so there were always risks involved for me. So starting Ellington Timepiece was challenging in the actions I had to do, but it was my passion, so I had to.

A few years after deciding to start Ellington Timepiece at age twenty-four, I'm still making big decisions that could have an impact on the business and my brand, like which factory I would use, where I would go for funding, which designs I would release, and what marketing I would focus on. As I've grown the business, the decisions have been bigger and more daunting, but these are the decisions you have to make.

I've been lucky enough to have a really supportive family giving me emotional support along the way. I have a close relationship with my dad. He has always been there for me, but particularly when I had anxiety in my teens, it seemed like he was the only one who really understood what I was going through. He'd been in business himself, so for some of the decisions I've had to make, I've gone back to him for his opinion because I trust him 100 per cent.

Who has influenced your decisions?

My dad and grandad have been big influences for me. They both had their own businesses. For instance, my dad will understand things I don't because I'm still learning. When I've asked for professional help, I got help from Five Lamps, a small business support organisation. They were the very first people I spoke to when I started my business, and as I've grown and as the business has grown, I've met new people with different expertise in different fields, so the decisions I've made have at time been influenced by the information I get from these new connections.

I couldn't give this résumé of influence without mentioning Adam

Hillier from Hillier Jewellers, who were the first to stock my watches. He helped me make decisions on designs, materials, and price point. So I've found it really valuable to find people whom you trust and believe are giving you the right information, and finding people who have your best interests at heart is difficult but not impossible. I feel like I've been lucky because more often than not, when I tell people my story and about my products, I get genuine offers of support, help, and advice. I do believe that these people have my interests at heart.

Did you consciously want to be the best at what you do?

I am my own worst critic, and I think I am a bit of a perfectionist in everything I do from taking design of my products, photography for marketing, sales, and everything in between. I will spend hours and hours obsessing over the smallest details. When a customer purchases a watch, I personally check everything about it before it goes out, from removing dust particles from the watch itself and the material inside the box. I check the authenticity certificate for accuracy and verify the wax seal that secures its envelope has the letter A the correct way round. Only when I've personally done this level of quality control will I release the watch. If you're not 100 per cent committed to something, you have to ask yourself, "Am I doing it properly, and why am I doing it at all?" I want to be the best I can, and I try to show that through my products.

Is what you do an effort?

I really love the process for creating the designs. That's the exciting bit. The effort is getting my products through the door, so things like going through customs when my products arrive from the manufacturer, arranging transport, and getting the products to the factory. So those kinds of things are huge efforts for me, which can be exhausting at times. I've been a one-woman army for the last two years. I did all of the photography and the website. I set up the payment gateway to the website, all of which I've never done before. So it's been an effort, but it's been a process where I've experienced both effort and enjoyment. For example, I have days where I finish the day and I look through my diary and see that the list of things

I wanted to complete has a line of ticks next to it. So that makes me feel happy and productive. But I'm only human and the same as everybody else, so there will be days where it can be a lot, so you have to take a step back and recognise that you need to take that little break.

So for me, the creativity is effortless. It's what I do naturally and really enjoy, but the logistics and background administrative processes are an effort. But there are people out there who are the reverse of that, so I think it's important for people to understand this and do what they're good at.

With my use of social media, I try not to sugar-coat the success, so think it's important to talk about the journey to success and the failures you will have. I think the rewards in business are great, and the struggle helps and makes you become a stronger person. In business, if you don't have the rejects and don't have the knockbacks and failures, you won't grow as a person, and you won't be prepared for the major setbacks that can happen.

Would you rather do something else?

In a way, no. I'm happy that I'm doing what I am right now, but I always try to look at the bigger picture and think to myself, "If I weren't doing this, what would I be doing?" So the answer is no, I'd prefer to continue doing what I'm doing now for as long as I can. I think that at fifteen, I was an actress. Then I became a barmaid from age nineteen to twenty and worked with animals full time, and now I'm a director of my own company and creating watches, which is something I thought I would never do, so I am very happy doing what I'm doing now.

How did you stay motivated through tough times?

I try to document as much as I can by taking photos through my journey because when I'm going through a difficult time, I use those records to remember how far I have actually come. It's so easy for people to feel deflated when things don't go the way they had expected and when you come so close to giving up because I've had those thoughts and feelings where I thought I wasn't doing a good enough job. I think you have to stop and pause for a moment and just reflect on what you've done to get to where you are at that moment. I sit and think about the day I decided to become self-employed and to start my own business, to sitting on my laptop creating a line of watches and back then looking at where I am today. I would have been so grateful to be where I am today, so I think that context helps a lot when things are tough.

What disciplines did you employ to achieve the success you have?

I need to maintain a level head and a clear train of thought. It's very easy when you're self-employed to get overwhelmed with what you need to do, so I use lists in my diary to structure my days and tick each item off as I go along. I also recommend prioritising your work because sometimes the things you have to do can be important but not urgent, and other times things can be urgent but not important. I have also had to sacrifice because in business, it's necessary. I can't remember the last time I went on a girls' holiday or went out and socialised in the way I used to when I was nineteen and before Ellington Timepiece. For a point of reference, I have had to make decisions, like "Do I buy a new piece of makeup?" or "Do I put that money toward buying advertising space on Instagram to boost my viewing and build my business?" Every little bit helps, and you need to make those sacrifices if you want to be successful in whatever you choose to do.

Does it ever get easier?

No. But it's no in a positive way. When I started, it was the smaller problems I had to solve, like where I start a factory, where I get the funding, where I do this, and where I do that. You grow as a person, so as your business grows, your decisions get bigger and harder to make. The hours get longer. It doesn't get easier in terms of time and money spent, but what you gain is valuable experience and a set of skills, and through that, the more conditioned you are to making bigger decisions. So I suppose the answer is both yes and no … sorry.

What are your top five tips for *Decision Point* readers?

As a young entrepreneur, the top tips I'd give to your readers are, first and foremost, focus on one task at a time; otherwise you won't be a finisher. Second, always aim to overdeliver. It will help your reputation in the long term. Third, take responsibility. We're only human, and people make mistakes, but hold your hands up early. You will grow quicker as a result. Fourth, arrive before everyone else and leave after everyone else. This is leading by example. Finally, set goals, or you will never achieve any.

Thomas Aldred, Ultramarathon Runner

What is your earliest memory of either thinking differently or wanting to do something different?

The origin is that I've always liked running for as long as I can remember. I have always been into sports, so it was never really a decision to do it. But I think what led me down the path of ultramarathons was after a few years into my army, my career having done normal physical events, but it was very much just a case of turning up to do them. I didn't really have to train at all. There were actually two specific catalysts that happened in close succession that really ignited my fire.

The first occurred when I was flicking through my Facebook feed. I have a lot of friends who I'd served with at various times, but there were two in particular I really didn't like. They had posted that they had just completed the Marathon des Sable. This internationally renowned ultramarathon was a real kudos to have on your running résumé.

I remember seeing them in their photos as they landed in Morocco, and the next thing you know, a week or so later, their status comes up that they had completed it. And I was so jealous because they'd done it. I didn't like them, and most of all I was angry at myself because I wasn't doing it. I distinctly remember the exact moment, and I was furious at myself.

Why did you want to do or be something different?

Not long after that, I deployed to Afghanistan for about eight and a half months, where I was based in quite a small compound just outside Kabul, with all of my usual freedoms severely restricted. I couldn't go out for runs other than laps of the compound, which wasn't very big, so that grew very, very monotonous. And it's not a great place to run anyway, so polluted with so much dust in the air. And so suddenly something I'd done my whole life, I'd always taken for granted, I couldn't do it the way I wanted. And so that was the point in my life, in 2014, where I knew I wanted to do something different. So by the time I came back from Afghanistan, I'd signed up for my first ultramarathon, and I was ready to appreciate running a lot more.

But also what's funny is that as soon as you sign up for something like that and as soon as you tell people, their reactions become really quite a satisfying sort of side effect of all of this. So when I somewhat thought about the answer, you try very hard not to come across as really egotistical because I'm not. I won't talk about running if I'm out with my wife and friends or because it is boring for some.

But when people hear about it, when people hear about what you've done in the past, you can see the look on their face, they think you're absolutely mad. And they also dismiss. "I could never do that. I'd never, ever do that." And so I really enjoy being able to sit back and go, "You know, yeah, OK." It is mad because it's sort of when you really put it how black and white it is.

What decisions have been the most difficult for you?

Yeah, it's actually a really easy answer. The hardest thing is just going to sign up for the event, especially if it's out of your comfort zone, because once you've signed up for it, you've crossed the Rubicon. You own it, and all of a sudden it's not something that you'd like to do. It's something you're going to do, and that stimulates everything that follows. You're not training for no reason. You're training for a specific purpose.

And at some point and for some races, everything is focused toward that purpose. So you can translate stuff you've got to do with work. Maybe you've got a really packed schedule. So you've got to get your workout done in the morning, and then you're doing this and doing that, but you go because you know you are going to be on your feet all day when you're running the ultramarathon. So this is preparing me for it, but all that comes back from the most difficult part, which is signing up.

And then it feeds into what I said before. If people then find out about it, it becomes a bit of a self-fulfilling prophecy, like, "Oh, what's your next race?" Well, I'm doing this, and I feel like I need to try to be straight. Yeah, but that's it. The hardest part is signing up for it over the year.

Who's influenced your decisions most?

Um, well, obviously the two people I mentioned before whom I didn't like. They do because I still think about it to this day. But then there's also a close friend, John Ford, whom I like very much and get along very well with. He also happens to be a very good runner a few years ago. He beat me every 100-kilometre race, and John being John doesn't let me forget that. On reflection, I made a lot of mistakes that day, so every time I'm getting ready for a race, when I'm getting into the proper race day mode, or when I'm on the start line, I think about John. He's become the symbol for when everything goes wrong and is always at the forefront of the mind. And actually it's quite a useful mental hook for me because even if I'm feeling amazing and I've trained train hard and feel super, I remember that day when John beat me, so I tell myself, "Don't let that happen again."

And it's that whole. It's a little bit sort of. Cliché, but it's that learning if something has gone wrong, looking at it and going that went wrong for reasons I can control, and that means if I can control them, then it won't happen again. Or if it does happen again, it's, you know, something you've not experienced before, and it's not necessarily your fault, and you're not haunted by it. But it does sit there in the back of your mind as the driving factor, that fear.

There's one more thing that really influences me. I'm interested in successful athletes, and when I was younger, I did quite a lot of boxing. Now I'm not very good at being punched in the face, but I loved all the training. And I got a good reputation for being a hard trainer. So as I as I got older, actually I found myself watching a lot of Floyd Mayweather, whether it be his fights or training and stuff like that.

And it's easy to put Mayweather as inspiration because he's probably the best ever. But actually, when I thought about it, what made Floyd Mayweather so good was all the work he did that really mattered was behind the scenes. So when the cameras were there, you'd see him go through his routines, and you'd see him talk and be this the character, Money Mayweather. But actually, his mantra was always hard work and dedication. His basic attributes were not complex. It is just hard work, and it is getting up, it's training, and that is transferable to running. And although I am not the Floyd Mayweather of ultramarathons by a long shot, you can have a lot of that dedication and hard work behind the scenes . You can be better. You can train when it's dark. You can find somewhere to train if you have limited space.

Did you consciously want to be the best at what you do?

It's interesting because the definition of what the best is. Whilst I've been on winning teams, I very rarely come first in a race because there is almost always someone who's faster than you are. But for me, it's more of a question of why you want to do it. And my answer is because I can, so I might as well give it my best, and that's it.

I have always been struck by the idea that actually when you're training for a big event, you're spending time on it, and you're giving your time to it. Actually after a while, the journey is the reward. The journey is the fun because the race itself is just a natural extension of the journey you've already been on. So instead of building it up to be this enormously insurmountable event, actually you've broken it down, you've gone through training, and you've peaked at the right time.

The training prepares you for the event, but actually finishing it is more important than anything else. Certainly with ultras, you finish the race and get the same medal as everyone else, but you also get that satisfaction. You get to post it on Facebook. You get to share it. Your wife gets to somewhat talk about you. And so is that winning? Is that a victory? Yes, I think it is. But I think that's very relative to what you set out to do.

Is what you do an effort?

Yes, of course, but then if it weren't an effort, then everybody would do it, and it wouldn't be special. But actually the efforts and preparation when you prepare for events, when you take part in the event itself, the privation, particularly in the build-up, actually sharpens your appreciation of everything else.

If your Friday night routine with your partner is to have a few beers and a takeaway pizza, well, I'll tell you something that if you've done any training in the morning and you've pushed yourself or pushed yourself that week, then that routine you have actually becomes a reward. And the beers taste much nicer, and the pizza goes down much better because you've earned it. And those little things we take for granted in our lives, you appreciate so much more. Because I run ten miles in the gym for two hours today, so yes, I'll take the pizza, and I'm going to have garlic bread.

But then at the same time, it's not an effort because the fear of turning up on the start line and not being prepared should outweigh the fear of not performing. Therefore this should give you motivation to get to it or motivation and some sort of inspiration to get to do it because the worst position to be in is unfit and out of shape at the start line.

Would you rather do anything else?

I'm addicted to it, and I couldn't stop it even if I tried. And that's the thing with exercise. It's a natural high and leads to the rush and sense of satisfaction afterwards, whether it be after a training session, a race, or when someone asks you, "Wow, you've just run a hundred kilometres," and I can respond with pride and say "I have!" It's a natural addiction. I think addiction is probably an overused word because there are negative connotations attached to it. But actually, I think if you're motivated and passionate about something, then you should repeat it.

How do you stayed motivated through the tough times?

So the fact that, you know, I was really angry at myself when I was in Northern Ireland because I hadn't done it [the Marathon Des Sables] and these two people whom I knew had. I still hear my good friend John giving me stick all the time. So that friendly rivalry helps me to get my training done when it's a bit harder to do it. But the other thing that motivates me is that you've already signed up for it. So this is going to happen, and you might as well train and prepare yourself so you can do yourself justice on the day. And the third one, as I said before, is that pizza and beer taste so much better after you've run ten miles in the morning.

What disciplines did you employ to achieve the success you have?

Preparation is essential. You're preparing not only your body for what's going to happen, you are testing your kit, trainers, shorts, and things like that, but also, most importantly, you're getting your mind ready. You're preparing your mind and getting used to the sensations you feel when you're going to be gone for a long time. So that preparation is essential.

I also use visualisation. There's a point of every ultramarathon or race I've done where I can think about the finish line, but I don't think about the finish line to suddenly relieve myself of all pain and suffering.

What you do is you go through. You start to visualize reaching the finish line, getting your medal and T-shirt, and then going to walk over to where the tents are to sit down. I'm going to have a protein shake and put my skins on. I'm going to phone my wife and have a shower. And then I see how I feel. Then I'm out of the tent, and I'll see where everyone else is. And that's exactly it.

But what I'm really looking forward to is feeling normal again. It's not having to worry about a race, so that is real, along with all the little things you yourself take for granted. It's not having aching feet or not smelling of Vaseline and deep heat. I wouldn't exchange that for anything. So when I'm having this visualisation at a halfway point, your mind can drift, and suddenly you find you've done another ten miles. And then you are into the last ten, fifteen plus five, and so on and so forth.

Does it ever get any easier?

No, it doesn't, but I can guarantee that when you get that finish and medal, it's time to find another event. And you'll find yourself wanting to do something else within a week easily. And so that doesn't get easier, but you do get used to the training, privation, and bits of your body hurting and rubbing. But that doesn't necessarily mean it's bad because it isn't actually. It's really fun.

What are your top five tips for *Decision Point* readers?

My top tips are really focused on running, but I think they are transferable in life.

First and foremost, I have a quote of my own that I like to share. There are people who love running, and there are people who haven't been running enough. So to expand on it, running is really natural. It's a natural thing that we have evolved to do, and even if you are out of shape, you hate it. You've had a bad experience. If you just run around the block and get the bug, before you know it, you'll be running around the block twice and so on and so forth, and it is just the exponential part of it starting with just moving and going from someone who doesn't like running to someone who does simply by running more.

The second one is that jealousy and frustration are really good motivators, and you should refer back to them, but you mustn't allow them to become all-consuming. Particularly with a race, when you're out there and running, the race is only about you. It can never be about anyone else. And although you may have the voices in your head, they may well be from people you don't like or experiences you've had in the past. You should fuel yourself with these emotions, but they can't consume you, and I use that as a metaphor for life.

My third tip is overtraining is the devil. You don't run a marathon to get to the start line. And so when you're signing up for something, when you're preparing for something, the last thing you should ever do is go from not doing very much to doing loads because you feel that's what you've got to do. Just break things down into smaller chunks.

My fourth point is to just sign up for the event. Even if it's just a pipe dream or a Saturday night "good idea" sign-up, the rest of it takes care of itself.

Finally, and I don't know, is this the most important one? In amateur running, success is completely relative, and it's relative to you. For example, my wife is not very much in the latter category of my two types of people. A few years ago, she ran a 10K and was really nervous before it, and obviously I met her at the finish line. And in terms of effort and achievement, her finishing a 10K is exactly the same as anything I've ever done, exactly the same, and I'd run fifty miles a few weeks before. So her success is relative, and I think people beat themselves up when they shouldn't. Don't compare yourself to anyone else. Just run your own race.

CHAPTER 8

Goal Setting: The 7W Framework

You can't go back and change the beginning, but you can
start where you are and change the ending.

—C. S. Lewis

Let's remind ourselves what we're talking about. A decision is just a
finished thought, and to have had that thought, you must have identified
a goal that led you to think about making a decision.

This chapter will be the capstone of those thoughts you may have been
having as you've read these pages. As we've discussed in previous chapters,
lots of people have thoughts and ideas all of the time. They believe they are
making decisions on what to do next in their lives, and I give credit where
it's due. Those same people act on those thoughts. But I would argue that
it's not a proper decision; it's not a finished thought. It's a passing idea,
where all the individuals see is the positive outcomes, the light but no
tunnel, and this is their biggest problem. There was never any real analysis
or thinking through the steps of the decision.

This chapter will guide you on how to identify your goals and take you
through my **7W framework**, a neat synthesis of the processes that have
led to all of my short-, medium-, and eventually longer-term goals, and I
fully believe this process will increase the chances of your goals becoming
a reality too.

Your goals are just that, yours! They are totally subjective and personal
to you. I hope that's clear by now and has been underpinned by the success
journeys we've followed in the interviews in chapter 7. Those journeys

offered you an insight into some of the highs and lows following a decision. But one thing was very clear to me. Despite those individuals being in different fields of expertise, they were all single-mindedly focused on their own interests. They weren't swayed by friends or colleagues. They fell in love with a vision and followed its path to their success. What unites these people and thousands of other successful individuals worldwide is setting goals. Not all of us are as naturally gifted as those in chapter 7, but for everyone else, myself included, a process of analysis can yield equally impressive results.

It's not unusual to draw a blank when trying to define your goals. It's normal, so don't worry. I find it much easier to consider my end states and to work backward, as we discussed previously. But you could also consider a few questions that might draw out the direction of your ultimate goal, and then we can get to work on identifying the specifics.

1. Who do you want to be? What is the ultimate vision you have for yourself?
2. What is the single biggest change you want to make in your life now?
3. What do you want to be known for?
4. What subjects do you want to master?
5. What subject do you know most about?
6. What subject do you want to know most about?
7. What makes you smile?
8. What frustrates you?
9. Who would you like to help? How would you like to help them?
10. Do you have artistic goals?
11. Do you prefer social interaction or quiet personal environments?
12. What training programs would you like to do?
13. Are there any qualifications you would like to have or need?
14. Do you want to change your job?
15. Do you want to start a business?
16. Do you want to learn a new skill?
17. Do you want to be proud of yourself?
18. What makes you anxious? How can you change it?
19. Who do you want to associate or network with?

20. What is the most important thing in your life?

Materially

There is nothing wrong with wanting things.

1. Where do you want to live?
2. What do you want to drive?
3. Who do you want to marry?
4. What do you want to earn?
5. Do you want to be famous?

Financial

1. What net worth do you want to have?
2. When do you want to retire?
3. Do you want to start your own business?
4. Do you want to be a millionaire?
5. Do you want to be a billionaire?

Look at the answers you've made previously. Out of all the answers you've considered or written down, which one resonates the strongest with you? Which one would you have if I could give it to you with the snap of my fingers?

Now add the next two most important on that list. This is your point of focus; this is the end state that you should be working toward. Well done! You've just identified your goals.

7W Framework

The 7W framework is and should only be there to guide your thoughts. It's not a set of hard and fast rules that must be followed, but I do consider the questions to be the most basic level questions you should be asking for quick identification and planning before you pursue your goals. So here they are:

1. Why do I want to change?
2. What do I want to change?
3. What is my ultimate goal?
4. What do I need to develop?
5. What resources do I need?
6. What is my timeline?
7. What disciplines do I need to guarantee success?

We'll expand on each question so we can challenge its relevance and see why we should ask it before the pursuit of your goals.

Why do I want to change?

This is really the secret to all self-help and personal development, and it's not by chance that why is the first question to ask. The why is the beating heart of the process. It's the question that has likely led you to think about making a change and will prevent procrastination from setting in and ultimately undermining the goal you had set for yourself.

The why keeps soldiers alive when deployed on combat operations overseas, why they fight that little bit harder, and why they march that little bit longer and survive day after day. Their why is that they want to see their loved ones again. The 'why' is the reason that the people in chapter 7 are doing what they love.

If we drill down to the fundamentals of why someone would want to become a millionaire, perhaps it's because they want a supercar, a mansion, or both. But why? Perhaps they don't want to have a mortgage anymore, but why? Perhaps they don't enjoy their jobs and don't want to have to go and do a job they hate. Why? Because they're not in control of their own life … ah, so it's the freedom they desire. Look back at chapter 7 and see if you see their whys. Nothing is more powerful.

I'll share with you my why. When I was growing up, we were poor. There was plenty of love in the family, and the family unit was tight, but for whatever the reason, there just was not any aspiration for greatness. I hated being told that I couldn't have something because we couldn't afford it. I wondered why all of the other kids had new clothes, toys, and games. I wondered why we never went into expensive-looking retail stores in town. I would make excuses at school about not having the latest trend, often by trying to act as if I weren't bothered or were somehow above the materiality of a new school bag or sports trainers. This was so powerful that to this day it has driven me to push myself, to work hard, not to limit myself to what others perceive as my limits, and ultimately to share my experiences in this book. Why do I want to change?

What do I want to change?

When you've found your why, listing the elements of what you want to change becomes much easier. It's exactly that, a list. I often use mind map doodles to list all of the components to my thoughts. It's easier for me. I don't have to worry about sense or logic. As soon as a thought enters my head (related or not), I draw a line to a new bubble and write it down. I mention that the thought can be related or unrelated, and that's because I believe the unconscious mind is a far more powerful untapped asset and data repository than the conscious mind, and there's a significant body of evidence to prove that. So while I can't know what my subconscious knows by its very definition, I do allow it the room to express, hence the reason to allow unrelated thoughts space on my mind maps. Insight can stem from the most unlikely and unexpected of places.

I wasn't academically gifted in school. I just couldn't understand why algebra or the history of the British monarchy was in any way going to positively influence my future. One of my earliest memories of considering what I wanted to do and where I wanted to work (using my crystal ball analogy) was that I wasn't certain where I wanted to work or what I wanted to do, but I did know that I wanted to wear a suit for work and I didn't want to get dirty. How I ended up in the army, I don't know! I'm kidding of course.

Subconsciously, as a child, I had associated traditional labouring work as lower paid and lower skilled and therefore not what I wanted to do. I wanted to wear a suit and be important. What do you want to change?

The army was a period that allowed me to understand who I was, to build on my why, and now it enabled me to identify what I wanted to change. The most significant thing I wanted to change was the benchmark that I and many other youngsters growing up in the 80s and 90s were measured by. Even now as I write this book, I am certain that the self-sabotaging nature of dreaming too small or setting the bar too low is the number-one factor in not achieving your dreams, closely followed by what your family and society expect from you.

The other listed items I wanted to change as soon as I was able to determine my own future was my environment. That decision took me to the army careers office in Wolverhampton, where I enlisted to give myself a broader experience of life and, more importantly for me at that time, an opportunity to break away from the neighbourhood and region where I was born.

In truth, I didn't think about this process in such a logical way back then. It was all intuitive to me. I was ready and accepting of any challenge I would face as I stepped out of my regional and social comfort zone.

I share this with you because I think it's important to understand that you don't have to have all of the answers. For me, it was a case of changing my benchmark, aspiring for more, and changing my environment. As I've developed a more detailed practice for self-reflection, my areas for development and change have become more specific. I've targeted health benefits (e.g., I quit smoking fifteen years ago), I've improved on the poor educational start I had, and I've changed my networks to suit my longer-term goals. What do you want to change?

What is my ultimate goal?

There's a clear distinction with your ultimate goal and the short- and medium-term goals that you'll set for yourself on your journey to success. Think of your ultimate goal as the final picture of success you can see when you close your eyes and imagine that everything has gone well and just the way you intended. This is just as important than your why.

If your ultimate goal is to win Olympic gold, I want you to imagine the feeling of crossing the finish line, jumping or throwing the furthest, and looking up at the crowds as your country's flag is being flown by all of your fans. Cameras are flashing, and people are gathering around you to congratulate you on an amazing race. You should feel your aching muscles as they have finally relaxed after the pre-race tension and in-race exertion.

Imagine putting on your trackside suit and sipping your bottle of water as you rehydrate and get your breath back. You're looking around in the crowd for your coach, family, and friends to celebrate with them. Imagine the months or even years of training it's taken to get to this point. Now imagine the formalities backstage as you prepare to walk out into the stadium once again to receive your medal, stepping onto the podium in first place, and the crowd roaring as you bow your head and are presented with your medal because they have followed you for your entire career, through the highs and lows to reach this point.

Drink this vision in. This is your ultimate goal and is what will keep procrastination at bay when you're not feeling as motivated as you know you should be. This is what separates gold medal winners from everyone else.

As a youngster, I had a picture in my mind of where I wanted to be and what I wanted to do when I grew up. It was very materialistic, but I was a young man with a desire to have a fast car, own my own home, and have lots of money. It was pretty vague, but it was enough of a vision to motivate me to get started on my journey for self-improvement. I've asked myself these questions, and my ultimate goals are even more detailed than the example of the athlete above. Each individual item I've purchased in my ultimate vision has been a journey with intricate detail.

For my chosen car(s), I've pictured myself arriving at the dealership in the morning, dressed comfortably with the knowledge that I have come to purchase my dream car. I have had casual discussions with the sales manager to see who the worst-performing salesperson has been because I know that I want to make sure he gets my business. From picking the colours and specifying what I want in the car is too simplistic. My vision extends to the coffee I drink during the visit, what's on the showroom music system as I look around, and what takes my wife's interest. I may be buying two cars that day!

My ultimate goal has evolved from the very material items of what you can see in my car purchase example previously to the more altruistic aspects of the goal. Writing this book is part of that ultimate goal. Giving back, sharing, and motivating others is part of my writing and coaching journey that will culminate in my ultimate goal, to reach a global audience and to influence and motivate those who need a guiding hand.

The short- and medium-term goals are not only useful but necessary. They are waypoints on your success journey and an opportunity for you to assess your progress at a particular date or time or whatever you've chosen as a metric. You can check you're still heading in the right direction, you're passing the exams you need to, or you're being promoted at work at the right times, or it could be that on reflection at these waypoints, your situation may have changed and you need to totally re-evaluate your approach. The short- to medium-term goals are, as I alluded to in chapter 4, a powerful tool in the kaizen philosophy.

As you achieve your short-term goals, you should give yourself a reward of some sort. There has to be some tangible benefit for you at each stage of your journey, as this will keep you motivated to keep going. If all you have is an ultimate goal that's going to be ten years in the making, then I'm almost certain that you will not reach that goal.

The short- to medium-term goals should be relevant and appropriate to your longer-term goal and also to you and your personality. If your ultimate goal is to gain a degree, then you might consider the individual courses that make up the degree as several medium-term goals and your shorter-term goals can be as simple as reading a piece text or writing a few paragraphs of an assignment you need to prepare for review.

Decision Point started out as one of my long-term goals, but as I wrote more and my ambition grew, it actually became a medium-term goal. Now in the longer term, I would like to write more books to complement the importance and structure in decision making that this book has demonstrated. I used short-term goals to help me write the book at a quicker pace by giving myself a small and easy-to-reach weekly writing targets.

In the beginning, I found it challenging because the targets were not specific enough. Instead of saying to myself that I would write a thousand words per week, I simply said that I would write a little each week. This lack of a defined daily or numerical target meant that I didn't hold myself to account each week and that if I did write a paragraph or two, then I was still making progress, albeit very slowly and slower than what I had envisioned for myself. The pace of my writing increased when I defined my daily writing target to five hundred words every day, and following my own advice, I made time to write those five hundred words. If I didn't write at 5:00 a.m. after I woke and had done my daily yoga practice, then I would write in the evening before bed. No music or no TV, it was dedicated writing time. I surpassed my target every day! What is your ultimate goal?

What do I need to develop?

Similar to question two, knowing what you want to change is closely linked and goes hand in glove with what you need to develop. To develop something means you already have it, so here you are identifying the assets and resources you can advance, improve, grow, leverage, or elaborate on. Let's assume you've answered the three previous questions in detail and you want to be a project manager in your field of expertise. When you finally become one, you want the biggest and most challenging projects.

You know you have all of the attributes to be a project manager, and you've listed some of them below:

1. Communication (written and oral)
2. Leadership
3. Negotiation
4. People management
5. Time management
6. Risk management
7. Budget management
8. Problem solving
9. Conflict management
10. Listening skills

Everything on this list you already have and can already use. You just want to get better at it. We know that these developments all represent short-term goals, and if grouped, they can represent medium-term goals.

If, like me, you struggle with your written communication, speak to your boss and ask if they will mentor you in writing project reports. Ask what they look for in the reports they receive and what a good and bad report looks like. Knowing this will give you a benchmark, which allows you to really understand how much or little development you really need.

If oral communication is the problem, then practice by doing short presentations. Again ask your boss or find a mentor whom you think will be able to help. It's an incredibly hard skill, and mastering it takes lots of practice.

Leadership, OK now this is a topic that has been studied for hundreds of years. There are literally thousands of books and academic papers on what defines a good and bad leader. I'm not going to cover that depth or breadth here, other than to say that if you're not a natural leader, perhaps you're an introvert by nature. All is not lost. Leadership traits can be learned and practised, and don't forget you're only developing the traits you need to become a great project manager.

Leadership starts with you. You must feel confident and good about yourself first before you can hope to lead and inspire others. Get yourself a new outfit and get your hair done. Do whatever you need to do to make **yourself** feel good about yourself. Then if it's appropriate, look for opportunities where you can take the initiative and lead a small project, team night out, or charity event. Again, this is all enhanced if you have a mentor and ask for help.

Negotiation does require confidence in yourself and knowledge of your parameters. Project management involves the collaborative input from a variety of stakeholders, all likely to have different agendas. But you know this, so a little trick here is to fully understand the purpose of the project, who is funding it, its outcomes, and a good analysis of your stakeholders. Armed with this information, you will be able to navigate challenges more successfully.

People, time, risk, and budget management are skills we all use every day. Making sure you get out of bed and to work on time is a clear demonstration of your ability to manage time. You manage risk every time you cross the road, and the same can be said for budget management when you do your weekly food shopping. When you arrive at work, you're managing people right from the start of your day. Development of these skills is thinking about how you take them to the next level and how you would manage your time if you had twice the amount of work but with a bigger (but tighter) budget. Also consider if you had a longer term-project and therefore more risks to it. You can do it. Just kaizen!

The secret to conflict management is listening. You've been there. You have two friends or colleagues who don't see eye to eye, but from an outside perspective, you can see exactly what the problem is. As a project manager, maintaining that professional distance as well as an approach that considers the whole project will enable you to deconflict issues early between stakeholders. These are one set of problems you're going to face over the course of the project, but armed with all of the enhanced skills you're developing, you'll have no issue in seeing your project through to success. What do I need to develop?

What resources do I need?

The previous question expanded on what you needed to develop those attributes or assets that you already owned. This question looks at the resources you don't already own. For this example, we'll look at a social media blogger and the resources they might need to start a YouTube channel.

We can agree that the subject matter they want to base their channel is self-help and motivation, and we can also assume that the goal is to produce a high-quality and professional-looking channel. At this stage, we can use a simple list, like we did in question two, to identify what we need:

1. Laptop (with an internet connection)
2. External microphone
3. Lighting
4. Recording equipment
5. Tripod/stabilizer
6. Script
7. Editing software
8. Courses and training
9. Marketing plan
10. Location/studio

With this list, you now have what you need to make your first video and share it with the world. But that's not the end of the story, is it? It's too easy for me to simply present a list of items that you'd need to make your amazing new YouTube channel. These things cost money, and for some of you (especially me when I was growing up), access to capital can be limited. On top of that I wouldn't be giving you any value. So let's revisit that list and see how we can achieve the same outcomes but on a much tighter budget.

1. **Laptop**
   Not essential. According to my research, there are over 3.5 billion smartphone users in the world today, and I'm betting you're one of them. Your smartphone will be your number-one essential tool to get you started instead of a laptop.

2. **External microphone**
   Not essential to get started. Guess what? You can use the microphone in your smartphone.

3. **Lighting**
   The sun is free! In your early vlogs, why not shoot your videos in the day? If you really want to shoot indoors, then choose a room in your house that's naturally bright. Turn on the overhead lights and sit yourself in the best position that will give you the look and feel you're after.

4. **Recording equipment**
   You guessed it. It's your smartphone

5. **Tripod/stabilizer**
   You can use anything at hand that you can prop your smartphone up against. If you need to elevate the smartphone for a better shot, then look around you and use what you can. Improvise.

6. **Script**
   Do you want one, or will you freestyle a discussion with a few notes to guide you? Either way, a script need not cost a penny.

7. **Editing software**

This isn't essential, but remain conscious that the goal is for a professionally edited YouTube video. Then we'll need to source it. A quick internet search returns a fruitful yield after typing in "free video editing software." Voila!

8. **Courses/training**

I'm convinced you can learn anything on the internet, and while Google is my go-to search engine, YouTube itself will provide a library of tutorials and tips videos that will teach you anything you need. Give it a go. Search for anything.

9. **Marketing plan**

You don't need an MBA to draw up your marketing plan. All you need is a pen and paper and to answer a few questions:

1. Who is my target market?
   1. How old are they?
   2. Where can I find them?
   3. What do they like?
   4. What don't they like?
   5. What do they need?

2. Who are my competitors?
   1. What are their strengths?
   2. What are their weaknesses?
   3. What are my opportunities?
   4. What makes me unique?
   5. Can I partner with anyone for mutual benefit?

3. What's my marketing budget?
   1. What marketing will I have to pay for?
   2. What marketing is free for me?
   3. How long is my marketing campaign?
   4. How do I measure marketing success?

4. What are my key performance indicators?

Answer these questions and summarise into a simple one- or two-page document, and you have your marketing plan … **free.**

10. **Location/Studio**

    Not essential. You can use any room in your home or an appropriate location outside. There may be noise in both of these options, but you could identify a time when it is quiet if that's appropriate to your video. If you happen to have a studio near you, there's no reason why you can't ask them for some free time when they're empty. What do you have to lose?

The content of both the first and second list isn't important. **What's important is the thought process you must go through and the frame of mind needed to carry you to your goals.** You have to **be solutions-focused. No problem is insurmountable.** I've learned lessons of mental strength from friends and colleagues over the years. Some of those lessons have been in the army, where giving up and failure simply isn't an option. Not everyone will be able to relate to that, but other friends of mine have used metaphors that are equally encouraging for me. You'll have heard them yourself, but think about them. Rome wasn't built in a day. Take your time. Don't beat yourself up if you're not proceeding as fast as you'd like to. The Egyptians built the Pyramids. (I like this one, especially when I'm trying to assemble flat-pack furniture.) What resources do I need?

What is my timeline?

The pursuit of your ultimate goal may be years away, so you need to schedule incremental waypoints at multiple stages. These are your short- and medium-term goals. If your goals are academic and let's say you want to be a part of the fight and eventual cure for a terminal illness, great. That's a suitably ambitious target and a worthy just cause for the good of our global society. Now let's frame this. You have this goal in mind, but you're only in high school, and being a research doctor just seems impossibly far away.

Before you start to think about the grades you need to get, you need to select the right courses that you'll need to get into college. The right college course is your springboard into medical school. So how long does this all take? Well, depending on what country you're in and the speed you are able to learn at, these times will be slightly different, but as an illustration they work.

1. High school: Five years
2. College: Three years
3. Medical university: Five-plus years

So in total, it will take you at least thirteen years to reach your goal, but remember the first five years are mandatory. So nothing extra is needed here other than getting a good foundation to your education and during the later years, preparing your mind for entry into college. College is a means to an end, a stepping-stone that you must complete. So treat it as such. Give yourself time to mix with others and widen your experiences because college is as much about transition into adulthood as it is certificates and diplomas. Finally as you enter university, the end is in sight. This will be a pleasure. You're learning the specific tools of your craft, so enjoy it.

I had a similar journey when I was a young soldier with aspirations of becoming an army officer as I explained in chapter 7. My planning timelines were a little less specific, as I was sure that I'd be serving in the military for several years, so I wasn't in a hurry. I intuitively knew that the time it would take to get me to Sandhurst was the great unknown because after I'd earned my place, I would be on a course just the same as everybody else.

Those pre-Sandhurst steps I had to go through, from application to walking through the gates of the academy, took approximately two years. I had expected it to take from twelve to eighteen months plus the year of training itself. I had planned to be an officer by the summer of 2006. I hit my medium-term goal. I was a commissioned officer, and guess what? The planning started all over again! How long would it take me to become a captain? Then how long would it take to be promoted to major?

The timelines for your goals are and should be tolerant to unforeseen or unplanned events, but you should think about them as it will motivate you in the short and medium term as you see progress at each of these waypoints. Imagine the confidence boost I got when I had earned my place at the Royal Military Academy Sandhurst. All of my preconceived doubts of my ability melted away, and I was on top of the world. I had just the right amount of energy to tackle the next step, the course itself.

I was good enough to get in, so I must have been good enough to pass the course. So those low points on tactical exercises in the early hours of the morning when I'd come back into our camp in the woods in the freezing British winter, I would remind myself that I signed up for this. It was a means to an end and all part of my plan. What is my timeline?

What disciplines do I need to guarantee success?

In chapter 4, we spoke at length about the disciplines you might need to succeed. I highlighted ten steps that should be employed to give yourself the best chance of success:

1. Wake up earlier and get more out of your day.
2. Be fit in body and fit in mind; be healthy.
3. Be honest with yourself.
4. Adapt what is useful and reject what is useless.
5. Practice, practice, practice.
6. Surround yourself with people who represent what you want to become.
7. Read.
8. Remind yourself of your goals daily.
9. Dress for success.
10. Meditate and reflect.

If you practice these disciplines, you are giving yourself the strongest possible chance of reaching your goals. Success is guaranteed. What disciplines do I need to guarantee success?

As you answer each of these seven questions, you will have a very clear understanding of your goals, why you want to achieve them, how you want to achieve them, and when you're going to achieve them. You have your plan mapped out, and the final words of advice I can offer before your action steps is to go at your goals with relentless persistence.

CHAPTER 9

Your Purpose

Knowing or not knowing what to do with your life is a problem shared with millions of people the world over. You don't need to have an answer for this question, but if you know what makes you happy, you will be one step closer to your life's purpose.

The world is in an ever-constant state of change, and you will never be younger than you are right now. *Decision Point* has broken down the key stages and questions you should ask yourself to help you make a well-informed, considered, and good decision. My aim in sharing my thoughts and experiences in *Decision Point* have all been with a view to help you answer that question.

It took me until I was in my thirties before I really knew what I wanted to do with my life, and my purpose has revealed itself to me as I've taken decisions at each stage of my development. I feel a sense of fulfilment in writing this book. I remain the same state-educated, low attention-spanned individual that struggled with focus. I wasn't an author until I wrote a book. I wasn't an academic until I graduated with my degrees. I wasn't a businessman until I started a business. Take the first steps, and use the tools in this book to guide thoughts. The paradox of knowledge is that it's one of only a few things that you can share and not lose anything in the process. You gain in so many ways the more you share the knowledge, so if you go on to share the information in *Decision Point*, you will be rewarded multiple times over.

The end of this book marks the beginning of your own success journey. Using the thoughts you've had and the notes you've made as you've turned each page, what are the conclusions you've come to in answering your own 7W questions set? You've arrived at your *decision point*!